PERFECT ACTS OF ARCHITECTURE

PERFECT ACTS OF ARCHITECTURE

BY JEFFREY KIPNIS

PREFACE BY TERENCE RILEY

THE MUSEUM OF MODERN ART, NEW YORK
WEXNER CENTER FOR THE ARTS, COLUMBUS

DISTRIBUTED BY HARRY N. ABRAMS, INC., NEW YORK

Published on the occasion of the exhibition *Perfect Acts of Architecture*, organized by Jeffrey Kipnis, Curator of Architecture and Design, Wexner Center for the Arts, The Ohio State University

Wexner Center for the Arts, The Ohio State University,
Columbus, Ohio, January 27—April 20, 2001

Heinz Architectural Center, Carnegie Museum of Art,
Pittsburgh, Pennsylvania, September 15, 2001—January 6, 2002

San Francisco Museum of Modern Art,
San Francisco, California, March 2—May 26, 2002

The AXA Gallery in association with The Museum of Modern Art,
New York, New York, August 15—October 19, 2002

The exhibition is presented with the support of the Greater
Columbus Arts Council and the Wexner Center Foundation.

This publication is supported by a generous grant from
Elise Jaffe and Jeffrey Brown.

Produced by the Department of Publications,
The Museum of Modern Art, New York
Edited by Laura Morris
Designed by Pascale Willi, xheight inc., New York
Production by Christina Grillo
Typeset in OCR-B, designed by Adrian Frutiger
Printed by Trifolio S.R.L., Verona, on 150 gsm Xenon Scheufelen

Library of Congress Control Number: 2001090089
ISBN: 0-87070-039-1 (MoMA/T & H)
ISBN: 0-8109-6222-5 (Abrams)

Published by The Museum of Modern Art, New York (www.moma.org), and
Wexner Center for the Arts, The Ohio State University (www.wexarts.org)

Distributed in the United States and Canada by Harry N. Abrams,
Inc., New York (www.abramsbooks.com). Distributed outside the
United States and Canada by Thames & Hudson, Ltd., London

Printed in Italy

Front cover: For full images, see (clockwise from upper left):
pp. 17, 49, 63, 169, 126, and 117. Back cover: For full images, see
(clockwise from upper left): pp. 33, 53, 105, 168, 153, and 118

CONTENTS

FOREWORD

SHERRI GELDIN
Director, Wexner Center for the Arts, Columbus

GLENN D. LOWRY
Director, The Museum of Modern Art, New York

The Museum of Modern Art and the Wexner Center for the Arts share a commitment to architecture as a vital component of our respective exhibition programs. Not only does architecture house our programs and shelter our public, but it also serves as a fascinating and reliable bellwether of contemporary culture. Accordingly, architecture is presented at both of our institutions as an integral part of broader cultural issues that engage the public at large as well as architects and other design professionals.

In addition, both of our institutions have demonstrated a commitment to architecture as the physical framework that defines and supports our programs. Peter Eisenman's work at the Wexner and Yoshio Taniguchi's designs for the new Museum of Modern Art are excellent examples of the role the architect can play in making a museum a critical forum for public understanding and enjoyment of art. Our commitment to architecture as a fundamental part of our respective programs is reconfirmed each and every day, as our buildings and the spaces within come alive with the activity for which they were designed.

It is particularly appropriate for the Wexner Center for the Arts and The Museum of Modern Art to collaborate on *Perfect Acts of Architecture*. Including significant loans from The Museum of Modern Art's collection, the exhibition has been commendably organized by the Wexner's Curator of Architecture and Design, Jeffrey Kipnis. At the start of this new century, architecture has once again become a subject of intense debate. As a mirror of the societies that produce it, contemporary architecture is now reflecting the myriad aspirations, conflicts, and challenges—within and outside the art world—that define our time and portend our future.

Special projects such as *Perfect Acts of Architecture* rely on the generosity of enlightened patrons, and we are enormously appreciative of their support. The Greater Columbus Arts Council and the Wexner Center Foundation provided the vital funding necessary to realize the exhibition. This book has been supported by a generous grant from Elise Jaffe and Jeffrey Brown, who recognize the enduring contribution a publication makes after the closing of an exhibition. We are grateful to them and to all who share in the cultural discourse such exhibitions and publications invite.

It is not clear that any graphic invention has had as much influence on architectural drawing as has Filippo Brunelleschi's early quattrocento demonstration of a reliable way of depicting perspectival space. The use of station point, vanishing point, and horizon would subsume the mechanics of the eye with the mechanics of drawing, allowing for a seamless expression of objects and the spaces around them.

It has been centuries since perspectival drawing lost its novelty. In the mid-nineteenth century, it also lost its claim to optimal verisimilitude to the supposedly more objective gaze of the camera. By the 1970s and 1980s, the practice of perspectival drawing had become more closely identified with professional renderers, whose skills were often employed to provide visual distraction from the banality of commercial architecture rather than to pursue architectural experimentation.

The six series of drawings in *Perfect Acts of Architecture* are responses to perspective as the dominant mode of architectural representation, employing collage, axonometry, superimposition, juxtaposition, and diagrams in various combinations. Furthermore, each series aspires to do more than depict various views of a building by constructing a narrative of some type that, in its sequence, tells us as much about the meaning of the architecture as its appearance. The temporal dimension implied by the narrative intermingles with the formal and spatial dimension, which opens up the projects to subjective content and interpretation in contradistinction to the purported "objectivity" of the perspectival view.

In the case of Bernard Tschumi's *The Manhattan Transcripts* or Rem Koolhaas's and Elia Zenghelis's *Exodus* project, the narrative exists in and around the architecture. In the first instance, it is a detective story; in the second, an urban cold-war myth that jump-cuts between Berlin and London. Cut-and-paste methods undermine the spatial and physical continuities suggested by perspectival drawing, calling to mind both cinematic and choreographic techniques.

Peter Eisenman's and Thom Mayne's house series both document the unfolding of particular aspects of the projects rather than depicting the resultant form. In Eisenman's drawings, the subject is the evolution of the concept itself. Like a chess diagram, various patterns emerge that are as much traces of a way of thinking as formal transformations. Mayne's project, on the other hand, demonstrates another type of pattern, one that arrives out of the imagined constructive process to reveal the house's fundamentally tectonic character.

The title of Daniel Libeskind's *Chamber Works: Architectural Meditations on Themes from Heraclitus* mixes musical and literary metaphors. Both kinds imply temporal dimensions, appearing in the works as a register of dissonant voices that rise and fall to an unseen score, their traces evident in the notational drawing. Libeskind's *Micromegas* seems equally to record simultaneous voices. In this instance, however, the score is no longer evident, resulting in a palpable, polyphonic mass.

In making his first depiction of Florence's baptistery, Brunelleschi himself recognized the limitations of his invention. To address those limitations, he added a sky of silver leaf, so that the clouds, the light, and their shifting environmental effects—all of which were outside the domain of perspectival drawing—could be represented alongside the spatial and formal qualities of the architecture. The drawings in *Perfect Acts of Architecture* likewise address not only the solidity of physical form but also the flow of architectural possibilities and spatial contingencies.

ACKNOWLEDGMENTS JEFFREY KIPNIS

Curator of Architecture and Design, Wexner Center for the Arts
Professor, Austin E. Knowlton School of Architecture,
The Ohio State University

No doubt as I soon become jaded to the process of mounting exhibitions, I will toss off acknowledgments with careless rote, hardly giving a thought to the people who do the work for which I take credit. I look forward to going through the motions, listing names and offering boilerplate homage, secure that, in truth, I not only did the most important work but all of the hard work. Finding stuff, getting it here, hanging it safely and securely, making it interesting to see, identifying it, taking care of it, returning it, paying for things, and all that pale when confronted with the exhausting, infinitely more arduous task of daydreaming about what would be fun to see on the walls and talking on the phone with friends to see if they want to come to a party.

Unfortunately, *Perfect Acts of Architecture* was my first show—for two years, from the moment it got on the schedule to the moment it opened, I stood frozen in traumatic immobility while everyone else did everything, including gently shuffling me from ward to ward with little toy telephones, paper, and crayons to keep me busy and help make me feel involved. So, on this one occasion only, I ask you to take me at my word when I offer the following, heartfelt thoughts of gratitude. Here goes:

Neither the *Perfect Acts of Architecture* exhibition nor this accompanying catalogue would have been possible without the cooperation of architects Peter Eisenman, Rem Koolhaas and Madelon Vriesendorp, Daniel Libeskind, Thom Mayne and Andrew Zago, and Bernard Tschumi. Their enthusiasm and gracious advice benefited the exhibition enormously. Studio Daniel Libeskind and Morphosis have my gratitude as lenders to the exhibition, along with Suzanne and Richard Frank; Shelly Einbinder and Andrew Zago; Centre Canadien d'Architecture/Canadian Centre for Architecture, Montreal; The Museum of Modern Art, New York; and the San Francisco Museum of Modern Art.

My Wexner Center colleagues devoted their skills and talents unstintingly to this endeavor from its inception, and I am grateful for the contributions of many more than I name in these brief acknowledgments; to those I omit, I ask forgiveness. I am indebted twice beyond expression to Sherri Geldin, Director, for her support and encouragement, and four times beyond measure to Annetta Massie, Associate Curator of Exhibitions, and Jill Davis, Manager of Exhibitions. Stephen Hunt, Graduate Associate, provided continuous, steadfast assistance and great conversation. Watching Registrar Joan Hendricks, former Assistant Registrar Robert Chaney, and Graduate Associate Cynthia Collins so deftly negotiate the labyrinthine intricacies of their arcane profession proved an awe-inspiring, jaw-dropping experience.

When it comes to exhibitions, trust me, installation is not everything, it is the only thing. David Bamber, Exhibition Designer, shaped the installation of *Perfect Acts of Architecture* perfectly as an elegant and integral part of *Suite Fantastique,* an ensemble of four interconnected design exhibitions. The installation team worked like an organism, each member making invaluable, creative contributions to the whole. It included Pug Heller, Assistant Exhibition Designer; Benjamin Knepper, Exhibition Designer; and James A. Scott, Chief Exhibition Designer. Jeffrey M. Packard,

Senior Graphic Designer, and Ann Bremner, Editor, worked effectively to communicate the exhibition's identity in graphics and text, despite my best efforts to thwart them at every turn. A special thanks to Greg Wilson, Frame Shop Coordinator at the San Francisco Museum of Modern Art, who built frames for works from another lender, so that all the frames in the Libeskind installation would perfectly match. There are good people and good institutions in the world.

I am gratified that the show travels to the Heinz Architectural Center of Pittsburgh's Carnegie Museum of Art, to the San Francisco Museum of Modern Art, and to The AXA Gallery in New York in association with The Museum of Modern Art. For this tour, thanks are due to Richard Armstrong, Director, Carnegie Museum of Art, and Joseph Rosa, Curator of Architecture, Heinz Architectural Center, Carnegie Museum of Art; David Ross, Director, and Aaron Betsky, former Curator of Architecture and Design, San Francisco Museum of Modern Art; Pari Stave, Director, The AXA Gallery; and Glenn D. Lowry, Director, The Museum of Modern Art, New York. The staffs at these institutions also have my sincere appreciation for their contributions.

The Museum of Modern Art produced this publication with the support of the Museum's Publisher, Michael Maegraith. In the Department of Publications, Laura Morris, Editor, brought sage advice, capable hands, and unflappable professionalism to her work with me, to which she was forced to add transcendent forbearance. Marc Sapir, Production Manager, made a commitment to the highest quality of reproduction, a promise brought to fruition—on time—by the unyielding forward momentum and prodigious attention to detail of Christina Grillo, Senior Production Assistant. Graphic designer Pascale Willi of xheight inc. demonstrated a lively, intelligent understanding of the material to the book's great advantage. Peter Reed, Curator, Department of Architecture and Design, served as facilitator for the publication and as liaison between the Wexner Center and The Museum of Modern Art throughout the catalogue's development. Peter's attentiveness and spontaneous interest in the material reinforced my confidence in the work, while, more importantly, reminding me that fun is in the details. So modest, Peter, that he will not consider that worth mentioning. I do.

I reserve these last thoughts for a few personal friends. As I mentioned, *Perfect Acts* joined three other exhibitions at the Wexner Center, whose principals made contributions by way of advice, opinion, support, and the very quality of their own work, which enhanced immeasurably the drawing show. To Mikon van Gastel of Imaginary Forces; Fabian Marcaccio and Greg Lynn, collaborators on that amazing architecture/painting hybrid *The Predator*; and Scott Burton, whom to this day I sorely miss, I extend special thanks. Also to Donna De Salvo, my first mentor, who kept making me rename the show until I got it right. And to Bev.

Finally, I want to recognize with particular care the efforts of Terence Riley and The Museum of Modern Art. Terry extended personal attention and unprecedented institutional support to this exhibition, nourishing it as he would his own. The very existence of this volume, though only the tip of the iceberg, is testament to his extraordinary consideration. Terry and the Museum could have done far less for this exhibition and still deserve unbounded accolades; instead, they did everything anyone could imagine and more. I won't forget it.

AN INTRODUCTION TO A PERFECT ACT JEFFREY KIPNIS

The history of architectural drawing as an end in itself, as a fully
realized, self-sufficient work of architecture rather than a subordinate
representation, is well settled. For centuries, architectural drawings'
intrinsic qualities have attracted admirers. More importantly, from Filippo
Brunelleschi's mechanization of perspective to Joseph Gandy's *The Bank of
England in Ruins* to the crystallization of Modernism in Ludwig Mies van der
Rohe's Berlin skyscraper projects, architecture is punctuated by instances
of graphic works that in and of themselves have altered fundamentally the
course of the discipline. Innovations in projective geometry and pictorial
technique have transcended the problem of representation and proved to
be effective design tools, the graphic appeal of their rigor and complexity
adding tang to the resulting buildings. More evocative drawings such as
Le Corbusier's Maison Dom-Ino perspective and Ron Herron's *Walking City* have
offered conceptual inspiration that transformed subsequent building with as
much force. Thus, the architectural drawing as end work can function in any
of three ways: as an innovative design tool, as the articulation of a new
direction, or as a creation of consummate artistic merit. Put simply, a
perfect act of architecture achieves all three at once.
    Equally settled are the influences that led to this particular gathering
of "perfect acts of architecture" by Peter Eisenman, Rem Koolhaas and
company, Daniel Libeskind, Thom Mayne, and Bernard Tschumi. By the early
1960s, an experimental itch, stimulated by innovations in the arts and film,
found purchase in architectural speculation on paper. The cultural climate
of sex, drugs, and rock and roll stoked itch into urge, further fueled by
the social roilings of the American civil-rights movement and Vietnam War
protests and of the brainier philosophical-political upheavals under
way in Europe, culminating in the May 1968 strikes. A general distrust of
all received institutions and social conventions abounded, manifest in
architecture as a distrust for type and program. This skepticism took on
a buoyant, optimistic haze with the conviction that the bankrupt heritage—
and its collaborating architecture—would soon, and easily, be replaced by
a more radical, democratic, free, uninhibited world.
    In the early 1970s, a sluggish world economy that all but curtailed new
building moved the most talented architects into teaching positions in
schools, where the graphic experimentation already afoot condensed into a
primary mode of research. Among the many schools important at the time,
the Architectural Association of London and the Institute for Architecture
and Urban Studies in New York became primary incubators. In the academy,
architects encountered a turbulent intellectual scene filled with passionate
debates emerging from philosophy, film theory, linguistics, literary
criticism, and social thought. Thus did forces of history conspire to set
the stage for an eruption of "paper architecture" of incomparable beauty,
range, brilliance, and depth.
    Action-minded Architectural Association types such as Koolhaas and
Tschumi hoped to deliver architecture as a tool for radical social and
political reinvention by using it to nourish unexpected events, with film

providing an alluring model. Pasolini shooting handheld on the streets, Nêmec documenting the Russian invasion of Czechoslovakia, Godard and Marker, Russ Myers, montage, jump cuts, sex, violence, real life, stars—film was cool as shit. It is no coincidence that Michelangelo Antonioni opened *Blowup* with a car full of Architectural Association students/hippies carousing through London on their way to see Alison and Peter Smithson's radical new building for *The Economist*.

Others focused more on the loss of meaning: Libeskind through an esoteric plunge into the phenomenology of architectural consciousness and process, Eisenman by a cerebral journey through the arcana of structural and poststructural linguistics, and Mayne more intuitively, following his fascination with technology and the relationship between the individual and the collective.

Yet, though I do not dispute them, I rage against such settled histories; they feel like dead light. I love when subsequent events unsettle origins, not by revisionist overturning or debunking but by discovering in them unexpected latencies and untapped potentials. The exaggerated chiaroscuro of Georges de La Tour's paintings, once considered by connoisseurs to be too theatrical for good taste, gained belated admiration in a world grown accustomed to artificial light. Likewise, each of the drawings in the exhibition, executed just at the cusp of the revolution of the computer-aided design process, uncannily anticipated in its themes and techniques the profound impact of that technological development. Witness the Photoshop quality of Koolhaas's and Elia Zenghelis's *Exodus* collages, the overlayered drawing of Mayne's Sixth Street House, and the Boolean processes of Eisenman's House VI.

Thus, when I conceived the exhibition, I conspired to commit three curatorial conceits. I would choose from a vast, rich fisc of worthy end-work drawings a small group to anoint not only as the very best but as perfect. Secondly, I would withhold from the exhibition as much historical information as I could, deferring it to this book and to a parallel set of extended critical essays on each set of drawings—a sort of reader's guide to this volume—which I plan to write, but probably never will. Finally, I would exhibit them in idiosyncratic installations and in odd juxtapositions with unconnected work from both their time and today. In Columbus, this plan became a suite of exhibitions encompassing the furniture of Scott Burton, film titles produced by the design firm Imaginary Forces, and *The Predator*, a digitally driven painting/architecture hybrid born out of a collaboration between painter Fabian Marcaccio and architect Greg Lynn.

All this done to see if these drawings could make their way into the world again anew, for a new audience, a new generation. I hoped these surprising arrangements would solicit unexpected effects, readings, and feelings. Some other of my favorite period works, Jimi Hendrix's *Electric Lady Land* and Stanley Kubrick's *2001: A Space Odyssey*, for example, have managed to resist historical patina. Why not my favorite drawings?

THE SCENE: London's Architectural Association 1970—72: a school awash in sex, drugs, and rock and roll, David Bowie hanging at the bar; flush to a person with experimental hysteria quickened by the visionary projects of Archigram, architecture's answer to the Beatles; galvanized, sort of, by the European action politics of May 1968; intoxicated by the spontaneous American love-urbanism of Woodstock and its shadow, the erotic violence of Altamont; edified by the froth of the rumors of French intellectual thought; drawn to design, to mod and Carnaby Street, and to antidesign, to the swagger of the infinite cities of Yona Friedman and Italy's Superstudio and Archizoom. Anything goes, everything goes. For studio, write a book if you want. Dance or piss your pants if you want. Even draw and make models if you want, long as they are "with it." Structure or codes or HVAC? Go to Switzerland.

THE CHARACTERS: Four students: wannabe screenwriter, wannabe journalist, wannabe famous, the seriously gifted young Dutch student Rem Koolhaas; his artist girlfriend Madelon Vriesendorp; a smoldering, brilliant mentor turned colleague, Greek architect Elia Zenghelis; his artist wife, Zoe Zenghelis. They call themselves "Dr. Caligari Cabinet of Metropolitan Architecture."

THE BACKGROUND: Koolhaas visits the Berlin Wall and declares, "Neither those in the West nor those in the East are free, only those trapped in the wall are truly free," an early instance of the journalistic device he would later perfect, the *mal mot* (for example, "the brutally serene landscape").

THE CATALYST: A competition for new visions of the city hosted by Italy's *Casabella* magazine.

THE PLOT: To reanimate architecture as an instrument of social and political invention by exploring its subversive role in the metropolis and its capacities to host fringe activities and stage unexpected events. Reject experimental architecture's knee-jerk habit of exploring new forms; instead, explore the generative possibilities of new programs expressed as R- and X-rated scripts. Tell the story of a select few who abandon the stultifying anesthesia of urban banality for a life of hedonist sensuality and discipline, staged in hysterical exaggerations of modern architecture and urbanism with huge block buildings and numbing grids.

THE CLIMAX: A work set in three equal registers: a scattershot set of emaciated, anemic parodies of traditional architectural drawing; a storyboard of colorful collages; and a text/script. A certain graphic incompetence becomes a talent. Collage, diagram, and storyboard become standard graphic practice. Promoted to full graphic status, text joins the fray. Architecture learns to appreciate the difference between events and programs.

THE AFTERMATH: *Exodus* wins a prize, but so does every entry. Hey, those were the days. Koolhaas uses the work as his Architectural Association thesis project. Three decades later, he wins the Academy Award for lifetime achievement.

REM KOOLHAAS AND ELIA ZENGHELIS WITH MADELON VRIESENDORP AND ZOE ZENGHELIS

EXODUS, OR THE VOLUNTARY PRISONERS OF ARCHITECTURE

1972

Prologue

PROLOGUE

Once, a city was divided in two parts.

One part became the Good Half, the other part the Bad Half.

The inhabitants of the Bad Half began to flock to the good part of the divided city, rapidly swelling into an urban exodus.

If this situation had been allowed to continue forever, the population of the Good Half would have doubled, while the Bad Half would have turned into a ghost town.

After all attempts to interrupt this undesirable migration had failed, the authorities of the bad part made desperate and savage use of architecture: they built a wall around the good part of the city, making it completely inaccessible to their subjects.

The Wall was a masterpiece.

Originally no more than some pathetic strings of barbed wire abruptly dropped on the imaginary line of the border, its psychological and symbolic effects were infinitely more powerful than its physical appearance.

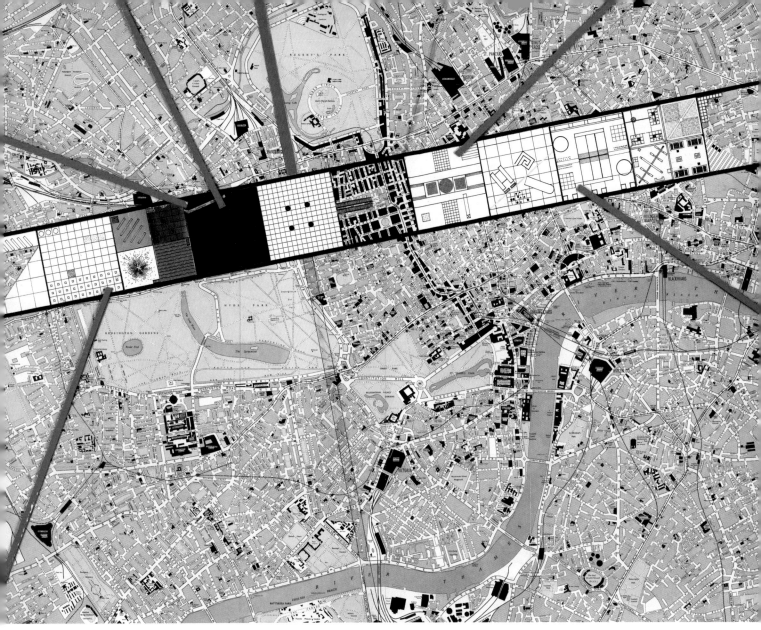

The Strip

The Good Half, now glimpsed only over the forbidding obstacle from an agonizing distance, became even more irresistible.

Those trapped, left behind in the gloomy Bad Half, became obsessed with vain plans for escape. Hopelessness reigned supreme on the wrong side of the Wall.

As so often before in this history of mankind, architecture was the guilty instrument of despair.

ARCHITECTURE

It is possible to imagine a mirror image of this terrifying architecture, a force as intense and devastating but used instead in the service of positive intentions.

Division, isolation, inequality, aggression, destruction, all the negative aspects of the Wall, could be the ingredients of a new phenomenon: architectural warfare against undesirable conditions, in this case London. This would be an immodest architecture committed not to timid improvements but to the provision of totally desirable alternatives.

Exhausted Fugitives Led to Reception

   The inhabitants of this architecture, those strong enough to love it, would become its Voluntary Prisoners, ecstatic in the freedom of their architectural confines.
   Contrary to modern architecture and its desperate afterbirths, this new architecture is neither authoritarian nor hysterical: it is the hedonistic science of designing collective facilities that fully accommodate individual desires.
   From the outside this architecture is a sequence of serene monuments; the life inside produces a continuous state of ornamental frenzy and decorative delirium, an overdose of symbols.
   This will be an architecture that generates its own successors, miraculously curing architects of their masochism and self-hatred.

The Strip

THE VOLUNTARY PRISONERS
This study describes the steps that will have to be taken to establish an architectural oasis in the behavioral sink of London.

Suddenly, a strip of intense metropolitan desirability runs through the center of London. This Strip is like a runway, a landing strip for the new architecture of collective monuments. Two walls enclose and protect this zone to retain its integrity and to prevent any contamination of its surface by the cancerous organism that threatens to engulf it.

Soon, the first inmates beg for admission. Their number rapidly swells into an unstoppable flow.

We witness the Exodus of London.

Training the New Arrivals

The physical structure of the old town will not be able to stand the continuing competition of this new architectural presence. London as we know it will become a pack of ruins.

RECEPTION AREA
After crossing the Wall, exhausted fugitives are received by attentive wardens in a lobby between the Reception Area and the Wall. The consoling atmosphere of this waiting room is an architectural sigh of relief. The first step in the indoctrination program of the other side of the Wall is realized: the newcomers enter the Reception Area.
On arrival a spectacular welcome is given to all.
The activities inside the Reception Area require minimal training for new arrivals, which is only accomplished by overwhelming previously undernourished senses. The training is administered under the most hedonistic conditions: luxury and well-being.
The Reception Area is permanently crowded by amateurs who through their dealings exercise an inspired state of political inventiveness, which is echoed by the architecture. The senses are overwhelmed by thought.
The sole concerns of the participants are the present and the future of the Strip: they

The Reception Area

propose architectural refinements, extensions, strategies. Excited groups elaborate proposals in special rooms, while others continuously modify the model. The most contradictory programs fuse without compromise.

CENTRAL AREA
The roof of the Reception Area, accessible from the inside, is a high-altitude plateau from which both the decay of the old town and the physical splendor of the Strip can be experienced.
   From here, a gigantic escalator descends into a preserved fragment of the "old" London. These ancient buildings provide temporary accommodation for recent arrivals during their training period: the area is an environmental sluice.

CEREMONIAL SQUARE
The other (west) side of the roof is completely empty, except for the tower of the Jamming Station, which will protect the inhabitants of the Strip from electronic exposure to the rest of the world. This black square will accommodate a mixture of physical and mental exercises, a conceptual Olympics.

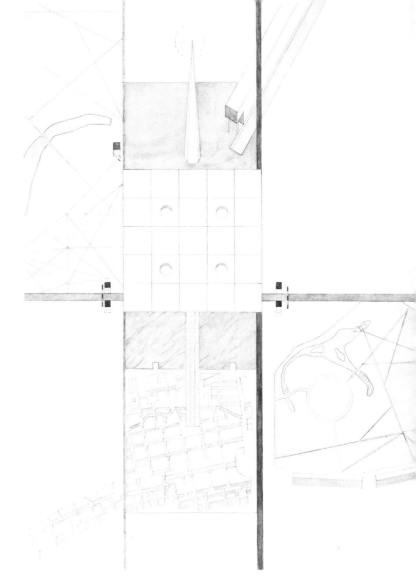

The Central Area

TIP OF THE STRIP
This is the frontline of the architectural warfare waged on the old London. Here, the merciless progress of the Strip performs a daily miracle; the corrective rage of the architecture is at its most intense. In a continuous confrontation with the old city, existing structures are destroyed by the new architecture, and trivial fights break out between the inmates of the old London and the Voluntary Prisoners of the Strip. Some monuments of the old civilization are incorporated into the zone after a rehabilitation of their questionable purposes and programs.

A model of the Strip, continuously modified through incoming information from the Reception Area, conveys strategies, plans, and instructions. Life in the building barracks at the Tip of the Strip can be hard, but the ongoing creation of this object leaves its builders exhausted with satisfaction.

THE PARK OF THE FOUR ELEMENTS
Divided into four square areas, the Park of the Four Elements disappears into the ground in four gigantic steps.

The first square, "Air," consists of several sunken pavilions overgrown with elaborate

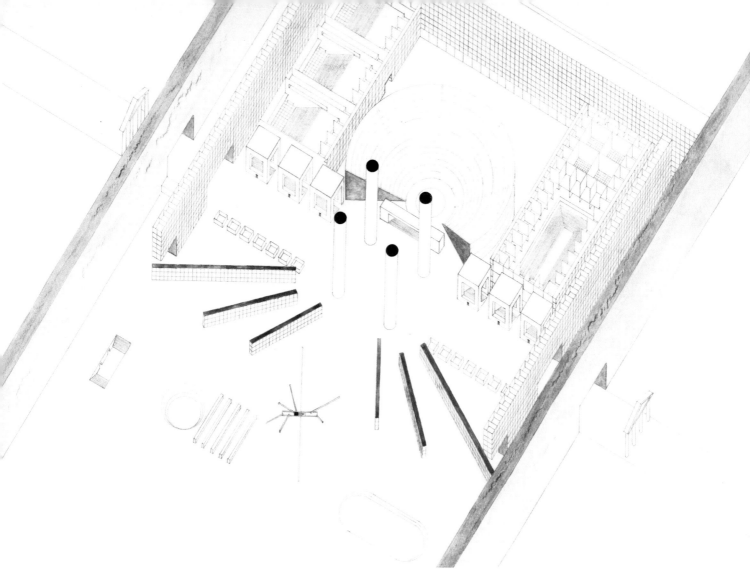

The Central Area

networks of ducts that emit various mixtures of gasses to create aromatic and hallucinogenic experiences. Through subtle variations in dosage, density, and perhaps even color, these volatile scented clouds can be modified or sustained like musical instruments.

Moods of exhilaration, depression, serenity, and receptivity can be evoked invisibly in programmed or improvised sequences and rhythms. Vertical air jets provide environmental protection above the pavilions.

Identical in size to the first square but sunken below surface level is "Desert," an artificial reconstruction of an Egyptian landscape, simulating its dizzying conditions: a pyramid, a small oasis, and the fire organ—a steel frame with innumerable outlets for flames of different intensity, color, and heat. It is played at night to provide a pyrotechnic spectacle visible from all parts of the Strip, a nocturnal sun.

At the end of four linear caves, mirage machines project images of desirable ideals. Those in the Desert who enter the tubes run to reach these beatific images. But actual contact can never be established: they run on a belt that moves in the opposite direction at a speed that increases as the distance between mirage and runner shrinks. The frustrated energies and desires will have to be channeled into sublimated activities. (The secret that the pyramid does not contain a treasure chamber will be kept forever.)

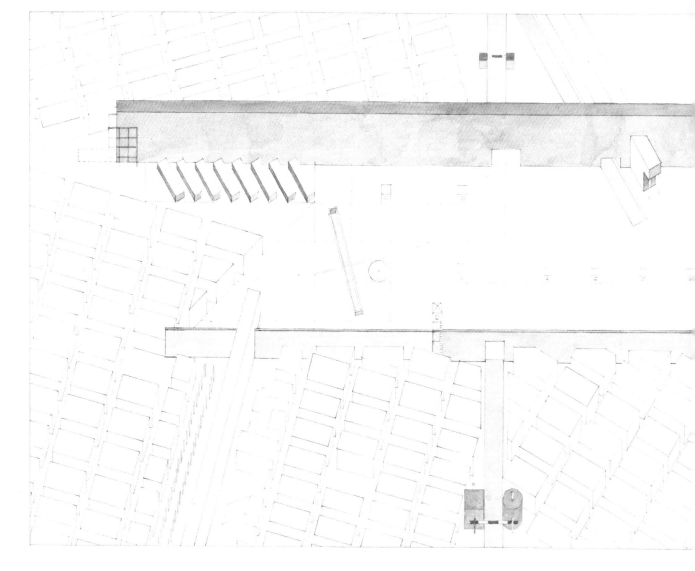

The Tip of the Strip

Deeper still into the earth is "Water," a pool whose surface is permanently agitated through the regular but variable movement of one of its walls, producing waves of sometimes gigantic proportions. This lake is the domain of some pleasure seekers, who have become completely addicted to the challenge of the waves. Day and night, the sounds of this interior sea serve as the acoustic background to the activities of the Strip.

The fourth square, at the bottom of the pit, "Earth," is occupied by a vaguely familiar mountain, its summit precisely level with the surface of the Strip. At the top, a group of sculptors debate whose bust to carve into the rock; but in the accelerated atmosphere of this prison, no one is important long enough for them ever to reach a conclusion.

The walls of the cavity repeat the past history of this location like a scar; part of a now-deserted Underground line is suspended in this void. Deep in the other walls, cave dwellings and cavernous meeting places are carved out to accommodate certain primordial mysteries.

After spiraling through the four squares, the wanderer is returned by an escalator to the surface.

SQUARE OF THE ARTS
Devoted to the accelerated creation, evolution, and exhibition of objects, the Square of the Arts is the Strip's industrial zone—an urban open space paved in a synthetic material that

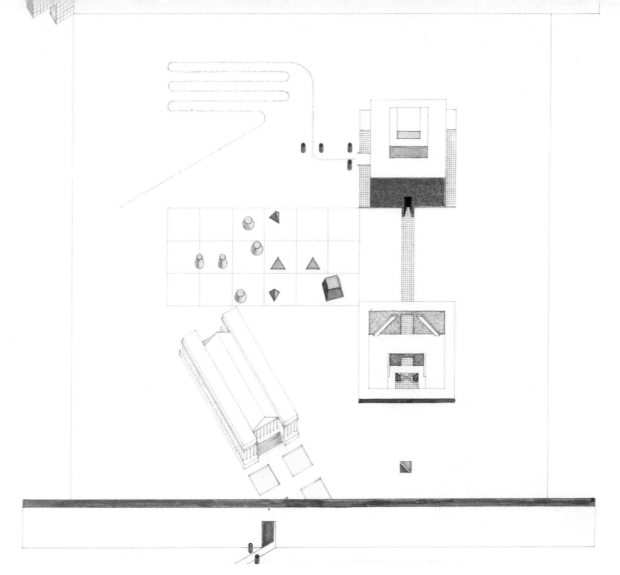

The Square of the Muses

offers a high degree of comfort to its users. Dispersed on this surface are the buildings where people go to satisfy their love for objects.

There are three major buildings on the Square. One is old; it has always been a museum. The other two were built by the Voluntary Prisoners. The first bulges from the surface; it was built with the materials of the second, which was carved out of the Square and is in fact the interior of the first. At first sight it is impossible to understand that these twin buildings are one, and that this is not a secret. Cooperatively forming an instrument for the indoctrination of the existing culture, they display the past in the only possible way: they expose memory by allowing its provocative vacuums to be filled with the explosive emotions of onlookers. They are a school.

The density and impenetrability of the first building intensifies the expectation of arriving students who wait outside its gates, while the apparent emptiness of the second provokes anxious suspense. The visitors, driven by an irresistible power, begin a journey down the escalators that link a series of enigmatic galleries into an exploration of the most mysterious corners of history. At the lowest gallery, they discover a bottomless interior; new galleries are under construction, filling, as completed, with unfamiliar

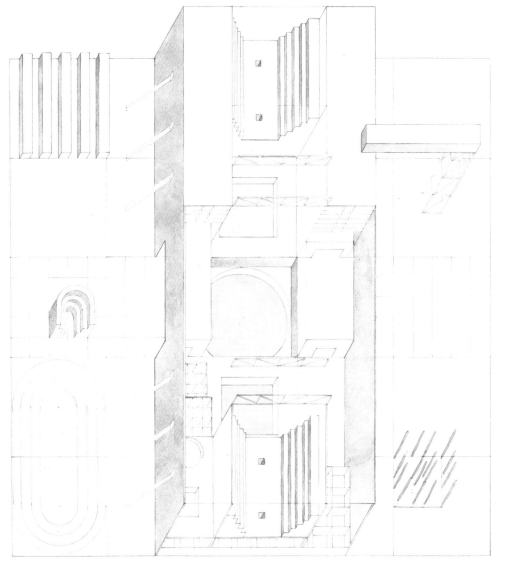
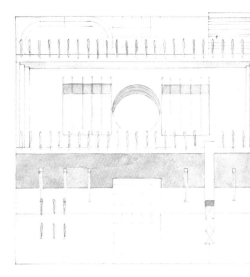

The Baths

works that emerge in a continuous flow from a tunnel that is seemingly connected to the old museum. Returning to the surface, the traces of this course are retained on the retina and transferred to certain parts of the brain.

The old building contains erased pictures of the past. The uninformed visitor's first impression is of an almost infinite number of empty frames, blank canvases, and vacant pedestals. Only those with knowledge acquired on the previous course can decipher the spectacle by projecting their memories onto these empty provocations: a continuous film of images, improvements, and accelerated versions of the history of art automatically produce new works, filling the space with recollections, modifications, and inventions.

Apart from these three main buildings, the only tangible exhibits in the Square are small buildings that resemble pawns on the grid of an ancient game. They are dropped like meteorites of unknown metaphysical meaning, waiting to be moved to the next intersection of the game; with each move they are further deciphered.

BATHS
The function of the Baths is to create and recycle private and public fantasies, to invent, test, and possibly introduce new forms of behavior. The building is a *social condenser*.

The Baths

It brings hidden motivations, desires, and impulses to the surface to be refined for recognition, provocation, and development.

The ground floor is an area of public action and display, a continuous parade of personalities and bodies, a stage for a cyclical dialectic between exhibitionism and spectatorship. It is an area for the observation and possible seduction of partners who will be invited to participate actively in private fantasies and the pursuit of desires.

The two long walls of the building consist of an infinite number of cells of various sizes to which individuals, couples, or groups can retire. These cells are equipped to encourage indulgence and to facilitate the realization of fantasies and social inventions; they invite all forms of interaction and exchange.

The public area/private cells sequence becomes a creative chain reaction. From the cells, successful performers or those confident about the validity and originality of their actions and proposals filter into the two arenas at both ends of the Baths. Finally, in the arena, they perform. The freshness and suggestiveness of these performances activate dormant parts of the brain and trigger a continuous explosion of ideas in the audience. Overcharged by this spectacle, the Voluntary Prisoners descend to the ground floor looking for those willing and able to work out new elaborations.

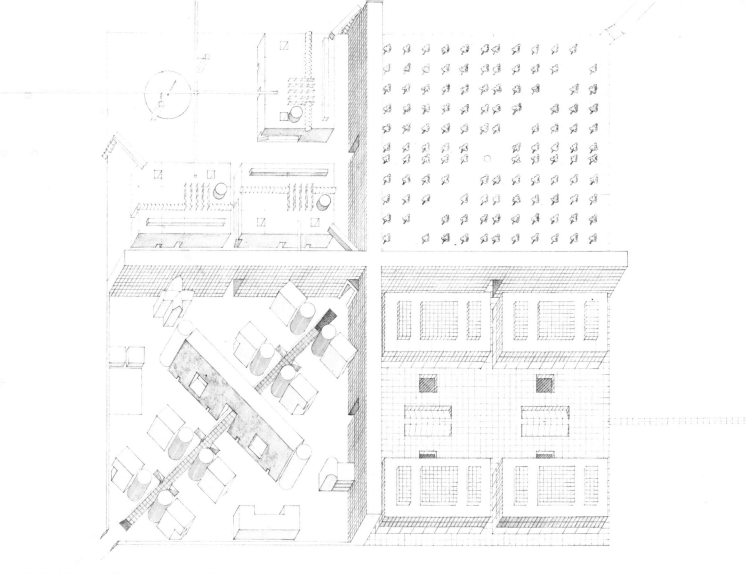

The Institute of Biological Transactions

INSTITUTE OF BIOLOGICAL TRANSACTIONS

The Institute sustains the Voluntary Prisoners through biological emergencies and physical and mental crises; it also demonstrates the harmless nature of mortality.

It is divided into four parts by a cruciform building. The first part, the hospital, contains the complete arsenal of modern healing, but is devoted to a radical deescalation of the medical process, to the abolition of the compulsive rage to heal. No forced heartbeats here, no chemical invasions, no sadistic extensions of life. This new strategy lowers the average life expectancy and with it, senility, physical decay, nausea, and exhaustion. In fact, patients here will be "healthy."

The hospital is a sequence of pavilions, each devoted to a particular disease. They are connected by a medical boulevard—a slow-moving belt that displays the sick in a continuous procession, with a group of dancing nurses in transparent uniforms, medical equipment disguised as totem poles, and rich perfumes that suppress the familiar stench of healing, in an almost festive atmosphere of operatic melodies.

Doctors select their patients from this belt, invite them to their individual pavilions, test their vitality, and almost playfully administer their (medical) knowledge. If they fail, the patient is returned to the conveyer; perhaps another doctor tries the patient, but it

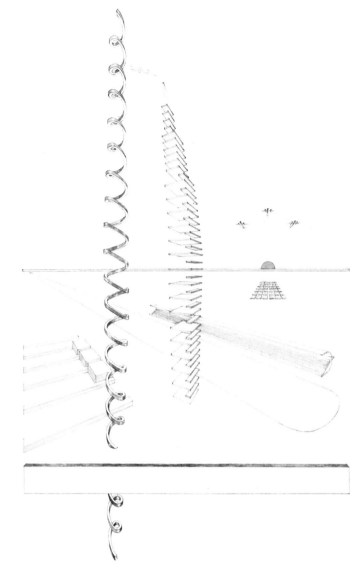

The Park of Aggression

soon becomes apparent that the belt leads beyond the pavilions, through the cruciform building, and straight into the cemetery.

The mood here is continuously festive. The same smells, the same ethereal dance, are made still more human by the contrast between the ruthlessly formal layout of the plots and the unnaturalness of the dark green shrubbery.

In another part of the square, the Three Palaces of Birth, there is a statistical balance between births and deaths. The physical proximity of these events suggests the consolation of a causal relationship between the two, a gentle relay. The lowering of the average life expectancy creates an ambitious urgency; it does not allow the luxuries of underexploited brains, the artificial prolongation of childishness or wasted adolescence. The Three Palaces of Birth will also care for babies, educating them and turning them into small adults who—at the earliest possible date—can actively participate in life in the Strip.

In the fourth part, mental patients will be on display as in former days, not as themselves but as part of a well-produced exhibition of their delusions, sustained by the most advanced technical equipment: an infinite number of Napoleons, Florence Nightingales, Einsteins, Jesus Christs, and Joans of Arc, all in their custom-made uniforms.

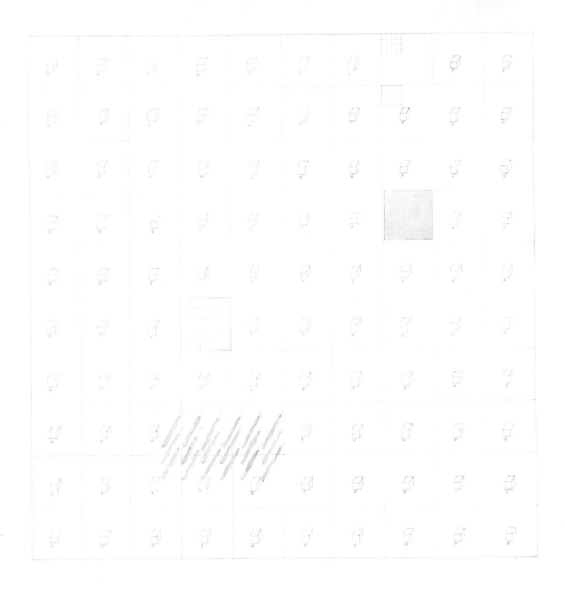

The Allotments

Finally, the cruciform building, which separates the four compartments, contains the archives—records of all vital facts, developments, and life incidents of past and present Prisoners. Bureaucracy, so often criticized for its passion for control, contempt for privacy, and moral blindness, guarantees the Prisoners a new kind of immortality: this statistical treasure, linked to the most imaginative computers, produces not only instant biographies of the dead in seconds, but also premature biographies of the living—mixtures of facts and ruthless extrapolations—used here as essential instruments for plotting a course and planning the future.

PARK OF AGGRESSION
In this recreational area, rudimentary structures were erected to correct and channel aggressive desires into creative confrontations. The unfolding ego/world dialectic generates the continuous emergence of conflicting ideologies. Their imposed coexistence invokes childish dreams and the desire to play. The Park is a reservoir of sustained tension waiting to be released, a gigantic playground of flexible dimensions to accommodate the Strip's only sport: aggression.

The Allotments

Here, conflicts are reenacted: the staged battles dissolve the corrosive hysteria of good manners. On an individual level, the Park is a sanatorium where patients recover from remnants of Old World infections: hypocrisy and genocide. The diagnoses provide richer forms of intercourse.

The most prominent edifices are the two towers. One is infinite, a continuous spiral; the other, consisting of 42 platforms, has a familiar architectural style. Magnetic fields between these towers create a tension that mirrors the psychological motivations of their users.

Entry to the Park is free, and performances are continuous; visitors arrive alone, in pairs, or in small groups. The aggressive confidence of the players compensates for the electrifying uncertainty about the safety of the square tower. Inside the tower are shelves containing cells where visitors withdraw to vent suppressed hatred, freely abusing each other.

But these private antagonists are also spectators: the shelves serve as viewing galleries which overlook the larger platforms of the tower, provoking visitors to join groups involved in unknown physical transactions below. As remnants of shyness are

The Allotments

overcome, visitors add their private energies to this incredibly demanding and mutant form of social behavior. In an agitated sleep, they ascend the tower; as they pierce each floor, their view of the activity below improves, and around the architecture of great height they experience an exhilarating new sensation of the unfolding spectacle.

As their tower leans forward, they push their antagonist into an abysmal fall through the relentless spiral of introspection. Its digestive movements consume excessive softness: it is the combustion chamber for the fat underneath the skin. The human missiles, helped by centrifugal acceleration, escape through a chosen opening in the walls of the spiral. They are objects of terrifying energy released into a trajectory of irresistible temptations.

The entire surface of the Park—the air above and the cavities below—becomes a full-scale battlefield. As the operations continue into the night they take on the appearance of hallucinatory celebrations against the backdrop of an abandoned world of calculated extermination and polite immobility.

As they return from their nocturnal adventure, the visitors celebrate their collective victories in a gigantic arena that crosses the Park diagonally.

"Exodus, or the Voluntary Prisoners of Architecture" – London 1972. Madelon Vriesendorp, Elia & Zoe Zenghelis, Rem Koolhaas

The Avowal

THE ALLOTMENTS

To recover in privacy from the demands of intense collectivism, each Voluntary Prisoner
has a small piece of land for private cultivation. The houses on these Allotments are
built from the most lush and expensive materials (marble, chromium, steel); they are
small palaces for the people. On a shamelessly subliminal level this simple architecture
succeeds in its secret ambition to instill gratitude and contentment.

The Allotments are well supervised so that both external and internal disturbances
can be avoided, or at least quickly suppressed. Media intake in this area is nil. Papers
are banned, radios mysteriously out-of-order, the whole concept of "news" ridiculed by
the patient devotion with which the plots are plowed; the surfaces are scrubbed, polished,
and embellished.

Time has been suppressed.

Nothing ever happens here, yet the air is heavy with exhilaration.

In his 1966 book *Cartesian Linguistics,* Noam Chomsky put the finishing touches on his decade-old theory that the "deep structure" of language allowed speakers to generate an infinite number of new sentences out of a finite vocabulary by means of a set of rules he called "transformational-generative" grammar. Eisenman, obsessed by a desire for an autonomous architecture liberated from quotidian obligations of function, comfort, and context, drew inspiration from Chomsky. He proposed that one could detach design from the mind-numbing convention of service and, instead, transform a finite set of elements according to generative rules. For example, walls, columns, and stairs could be treated not as functional or structural elements but as signs. Moreover, Eisenman claimed, this process-driven design would engender a critical architecture insofar as it diminished the presence of the architect—the principal vector of the bourgeois values that contemporary architecture should critique—and revealed architecture as a sui generis cultural language capable of speaking to the reflective intellect.

For more than a decade, Eisenman elaborated his ideas through a series of eleven houses. He worked out labyrinthine design processes for each, which entailed hundreds of diagrams and drawings. Indeed, he reconceptualized architectural drawing itself; the axonometric, for example, was no longer understood as a representation of spatial relations but as a syntax for semantic elements. "Building" became a matter of enlarging and rerendering certain drawings.

Eventually, a conflict became apparent to Eisenman: how could architecture be both autonomous and critical, that is, self-contained and self-referential yet engaged in a critical cultural exchange? In House VI, he attempted to resolve that question by extending the linguistic analogy, treating architecture not as a matter of architectural signs rearranged into new formal relations to be seen but into new texts to be read. Using a strictly Cartesian language, Eisenman wrote House VI as a text about the diagonal that passes through the center of a cube, a line that, although it is the subject, never explicitly appears in the design. Thus, autonomous because it remains within the generative grammar of architectural signs, critical because it revisits a history of habit in architecture that favors center and edge while ignoring the diagonal for cultural, not formal, reasons.

Upon finishing House VI, Eisenman prepared a set of drawings for publication that summarizes the crucial steps in the process and the emergence of the virtual diagonal, to which the antifunctional pair of green and red staircases in the last alludes (see p. 49). In these drawings-as-film, one watches three Cartesian units, a red grid, a blue grid, and a black/white cross of planes unfold and interact according to some obscure genetic program. House VI seems to emerge automatically, like a single cell's transformation into a multicelled organism. Though the rationale behind each step remains difficult to recover, the compelling sense of a deep logic driving the design launched both a generation of research into automatic processes and Eisenman's reputation.

PETER EISENMAN

HOUSE VI

c. 1976

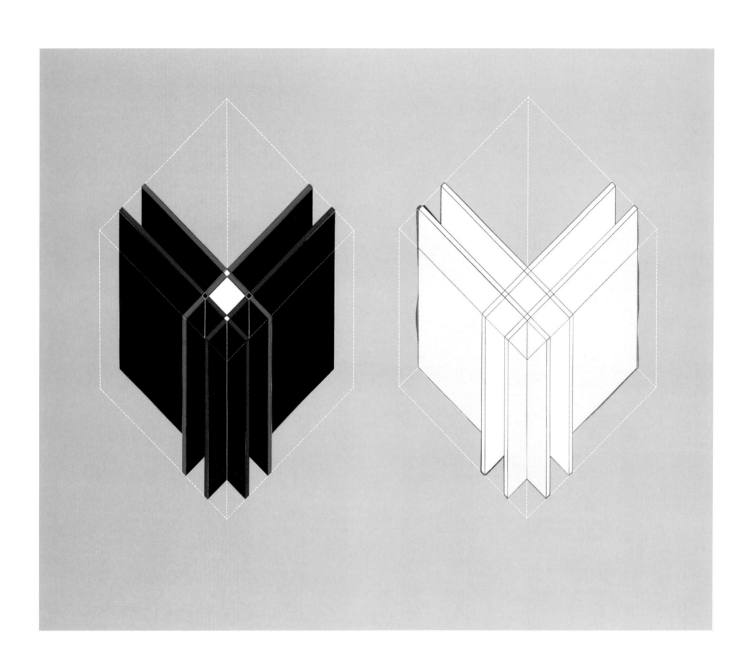

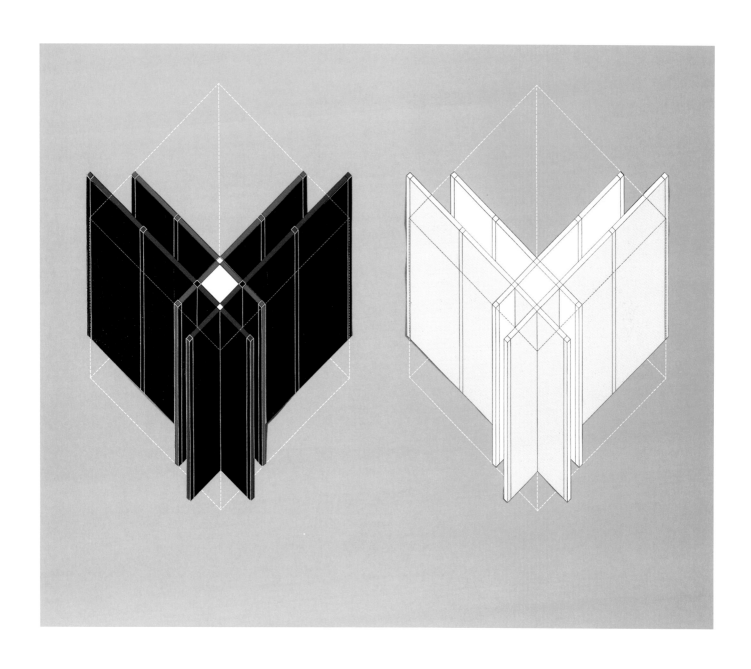

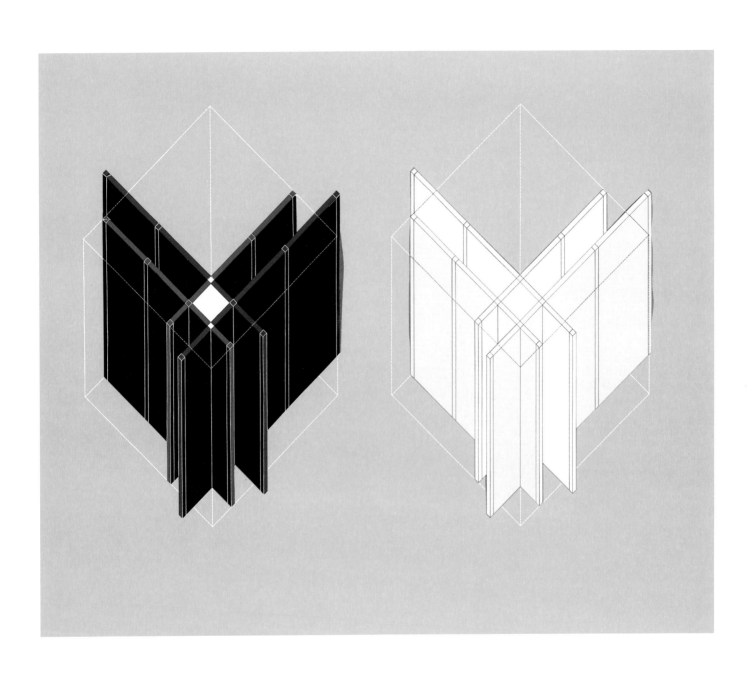

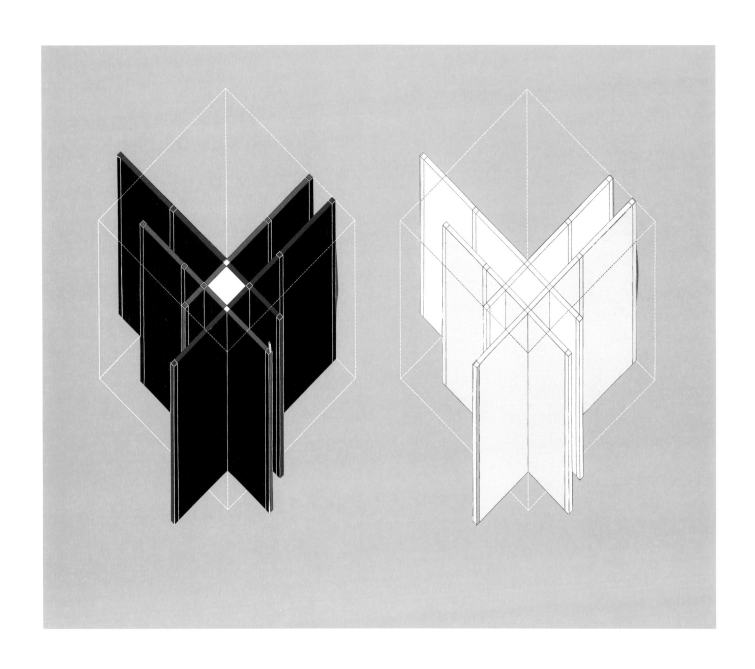

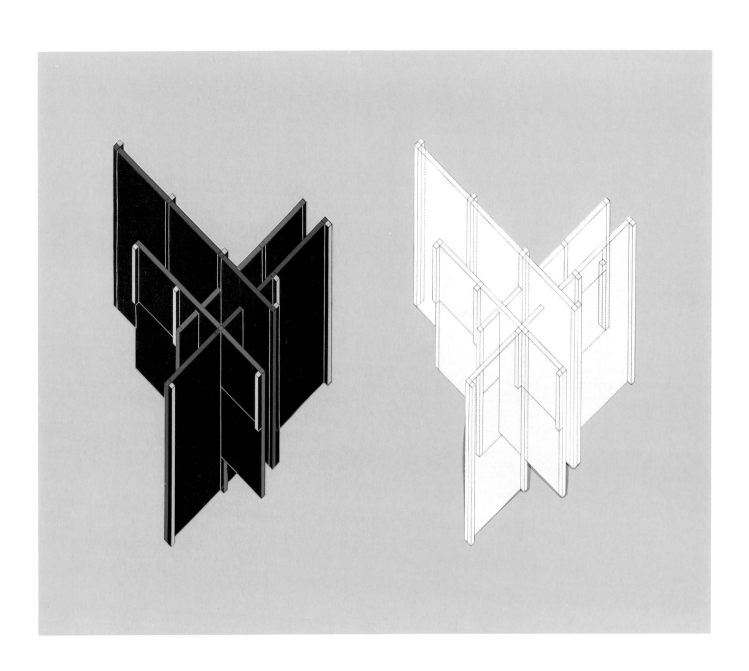

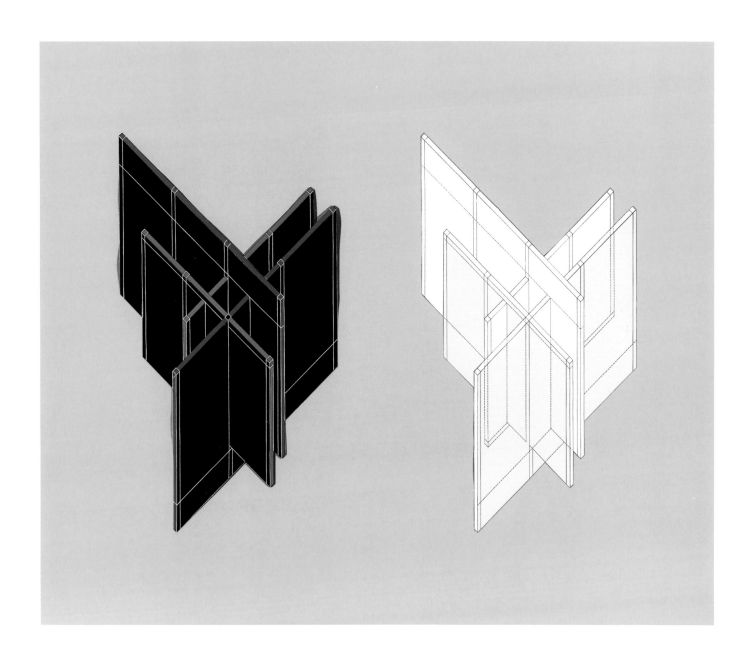

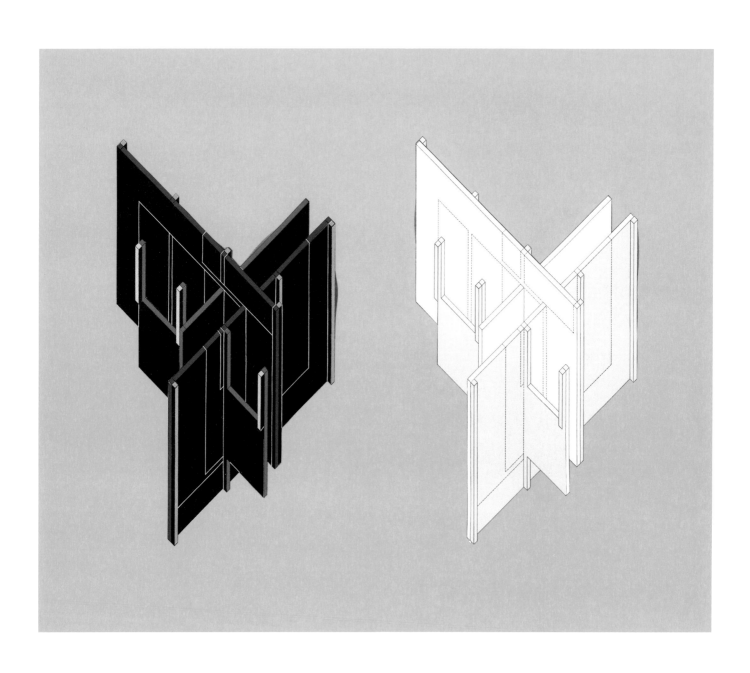

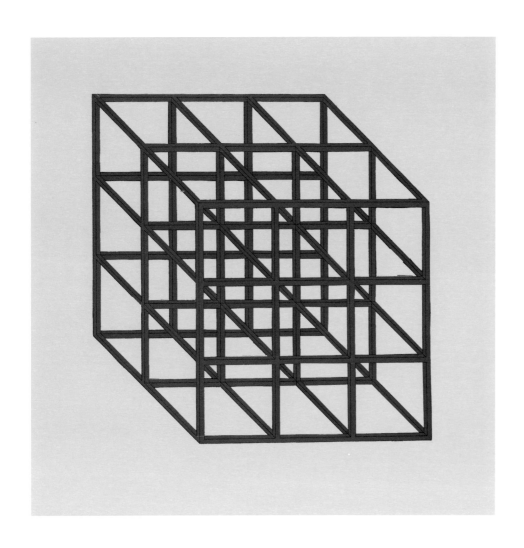

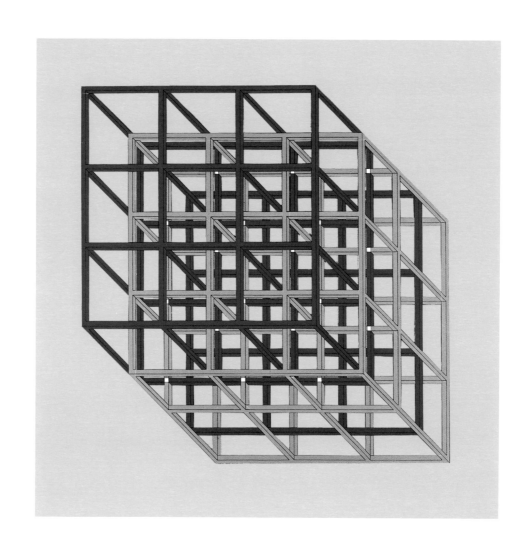

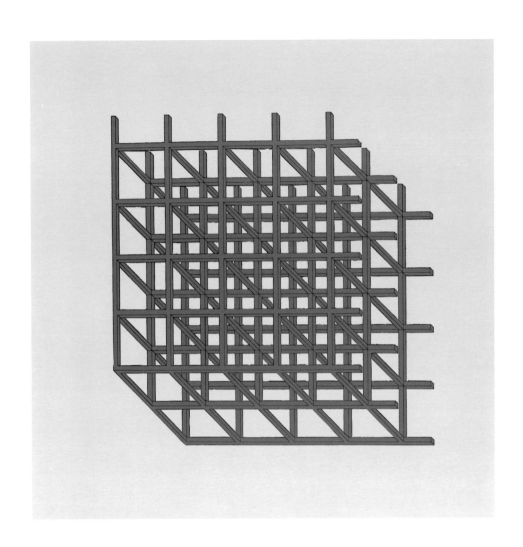

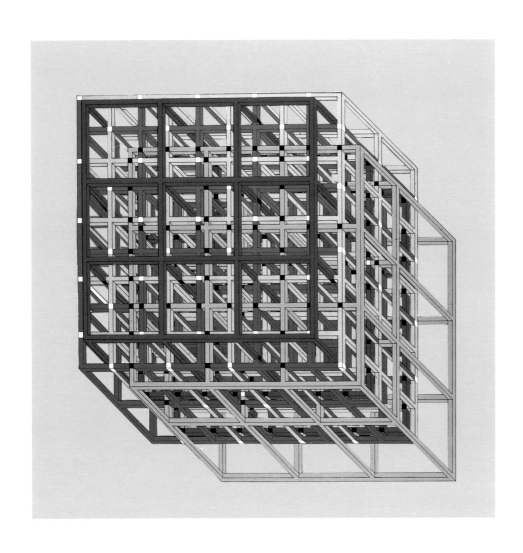

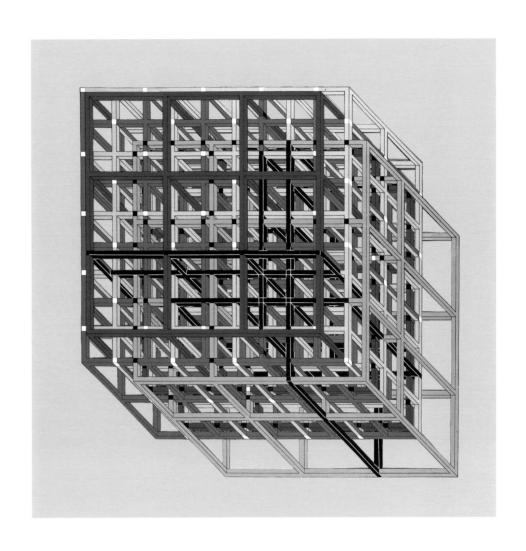

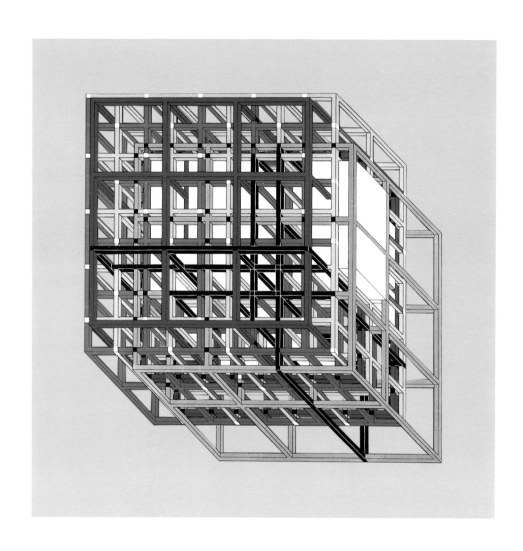

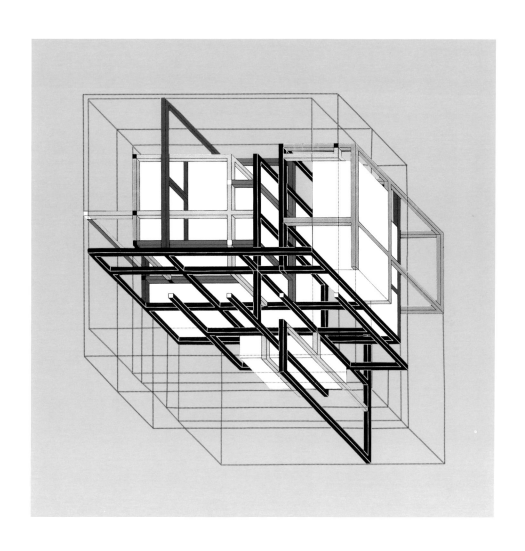

Stripped bare of affect, the blunt graphics of *The Manhattan Transcripts* lull us into a delusion of lucidity, even when their madness begins to leak, even, at last, when they burst into a flood of lunacy. As they stage this nightmare of wakefulness, this insane sanity, they are already more Manhattan than representations of it.

Executed between 1976 and 1981 for consecutive solo exhibitions, Tschumi's extended meditation, presented in four episodes, constitutes nothing short of a *Principia* of architectural sedition. On his way to New York, Tschumi studied the work of earlier revolutionaries. He also stockpiled conspiracies against architecture: assorted assaults by Bataille, Derrida, and Foucault; radical film techniques such as the jump cut, quick cut, and tracking shot; the antihero narratives of Godard; subversive agitations on the city by Archigram, Cedric Price, and others; and the prescriptions of Situationist Guy Debord, whose notions of *dérive* (drift) and *détournement* (deflection) constitute the sine qua non of the Transcripts.

Arriving in New York, the city abuzz with the graphic and notational experiments of Hejduk and others, Tschumi begins for the first time to draw. Here, he also encounters a group of artists, orbiting around curator Helene Winer, who are devoted to redeploying film tropes as visual art. Among them is Robert Longo, with whom Tschumi undertakes some early efforts in urban sabotage. Tschumi nods to that brief collaboration with an echo of Longo's *Men in the Cities* drawings in the final work of Episode 3 of *The Manhattan Transcripts*.

Over the course of the Transcripts, Tschumi digests his research, documenting it relentlessly through the severe limitations of uninflected citation, diagram, and hard-line architectural notation. By eschewing expressive technique, by resisting every urge to originality, by confining such volatile material within the straitjacket of conventional graphics, Tschumi causes it to detonate with a wholly original force. For over a decade, *The Manhattan Transcripts* would stand as the study nonpareil of transformative architectural graphics.

Each drawing in Episode 1 is based on a three-part device in which events, spaces, and movements are represented by, respectively, photographs, conventional architectural drawing, and motion diagrams. The device persists throughout the series, though it undergoes variation and weaves into larger, more complex matrices.

Episode 1: The Park constructs Central Park out of jump cuts as it tracks a murder mystery à la Antonioni's *Blowup*. *Episode 2: The Street (Border Crossing)* records a breathless *dérive* down Forty-Second Street. *Episode 3: The Tower (The Fall)* graphs the vertigo of a prisoner falling from a cell in a tower prison/asylum/hotel/office. Finally, *Episode 4: The Block* picks up the pieces and turns them into architecture, the punched sprocket windows reminding us of the sheer film of it all. Except for the buildings, photographed by the architect, the event snapshots in Episodes 1, 2, and 3 are excerpted from such magazines as *True Crime,* a genre of popular periodical now almost forgotten. The sports images in Episode 4 come from newspapers.

BERNARD TSCHUMI

THE MANHATTAN TRANSCRIPTS

1976—81

EPISODE 1: THE PARK

'They found the Transcripts
by accident. Just one little
tap and the wall split open,
revealing a lifetime's worth
of metropolitan pleasures—
pleasures that they had no
intention of giving up. So when
she threatened to run and tell
the authorities, they had no
alternative but to stop her.
And that's when the second
accident occurred—the accident
of murder. . . . They had to get
out of the Park—quick. But one
was tracked, by enemies he didn't
know—and didn't even see—until
it was too late. THE PARK.'

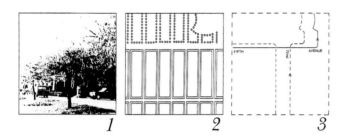

1   2   3

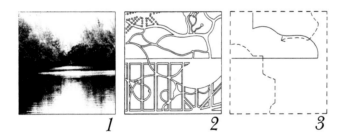

1   2   3

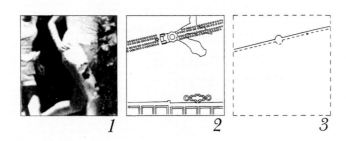

1   2   3

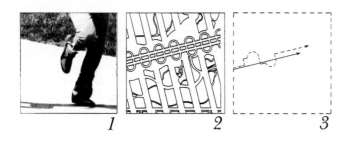

1   2   3

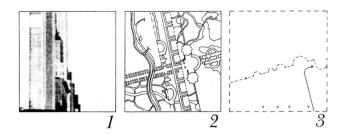

1   2   3

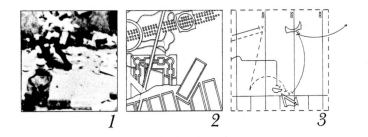

1   2   3

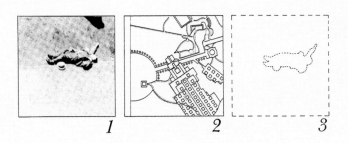

1   *2*   *3*

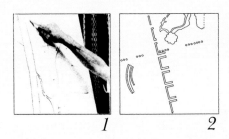

1   *2*

FEW CLUES AT SCENE

Police, Galvanized Into Action
at Midnight, Found Little on
Which to Base Search.

CRIME STARTLED WORLD

News Spread Quickly and the
Largest Detective Force in
History Was Mobilized.

3

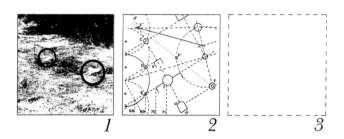

1 *2* *3*

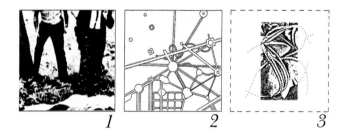

1 *2* *3*

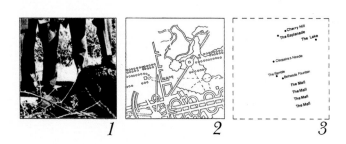

1 *2* *3*

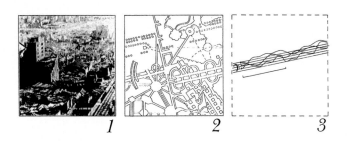

1 *2* *3*

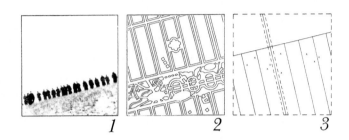

1   2   3

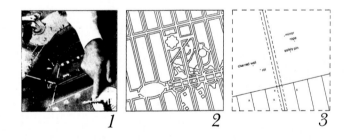

1   2   3

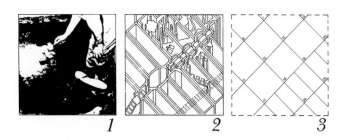

1   *2*   *3*

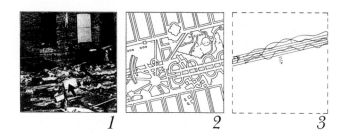

1   *2*   *3*

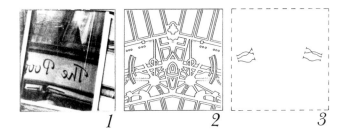

1   2   3

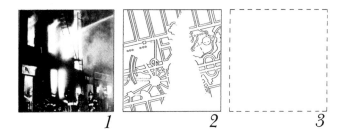

1   2   3

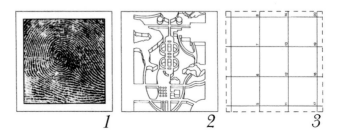

1   2   3

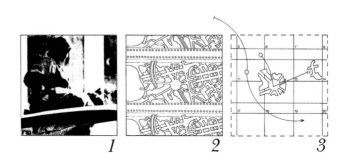

1   2   3

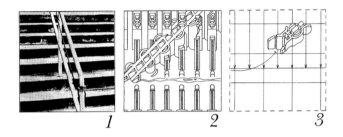

1   2   3

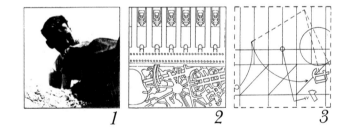

1   2   3

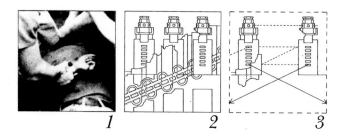

1   2   3

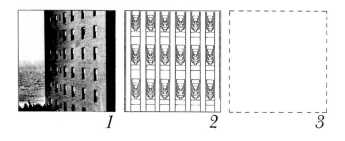

1   2   3

EPISODE 2: THE STREET (BORDER CROSSING)

'Border Crossing . . . Derelict
piers and luxury hotels,
junkies and detectives, cheap
whorehouses and gleaming
skyscrapers had all been part
of his world. So when he got
out of jail, he thought he
could pass safely from one
to the next . . . but then he
met her. To him, she was
an enigma—bold, shy, wanton,
and childlike in turn. From
the moment he saw her he
was a man possessed—possessed
by a woman who was beautiful
to look at, but lethal to
love. . . . THE STREET.'

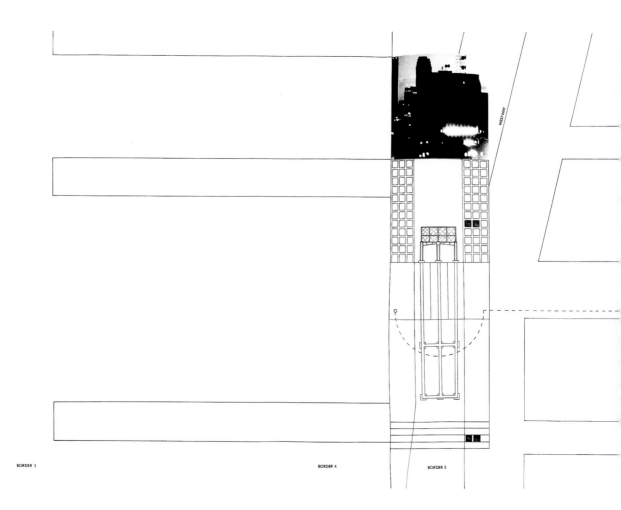

HUDSON

WESTWAY

BORDER 3

BORDER 4

BORDER 5

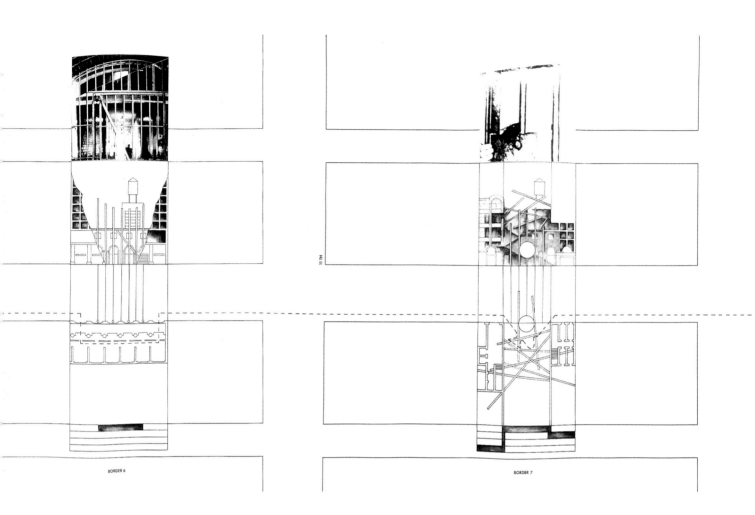

BORDER 6

BORDER 7

11 TH

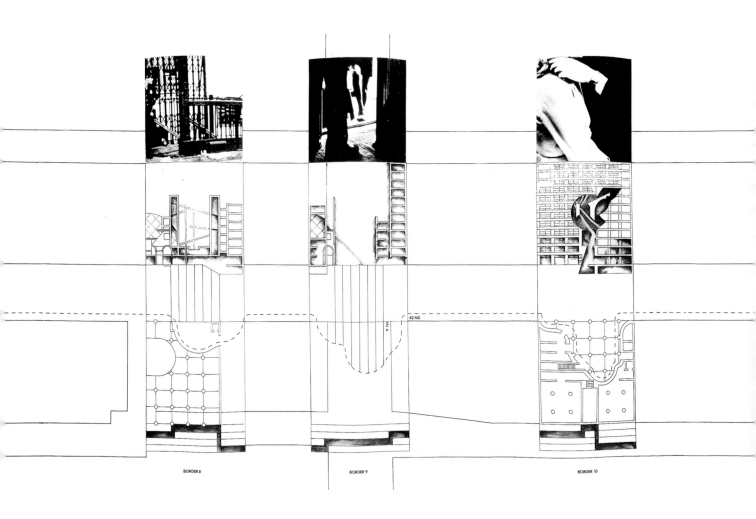

BORDER 8   BORDER 9   BORDER 10

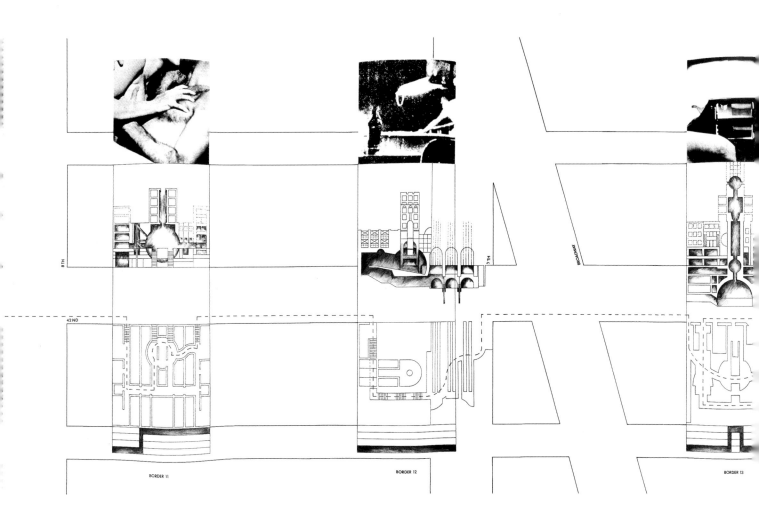

BORDER 11   BORDER 12   BORDER 13

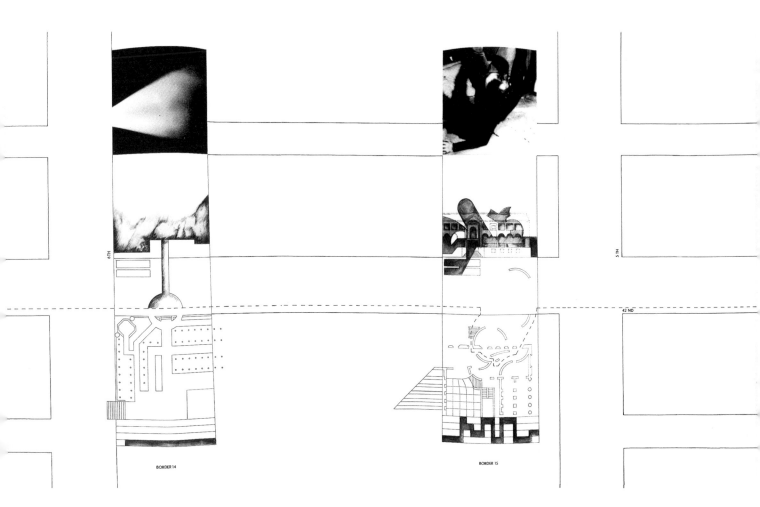

BORDER 14

BORDER 15

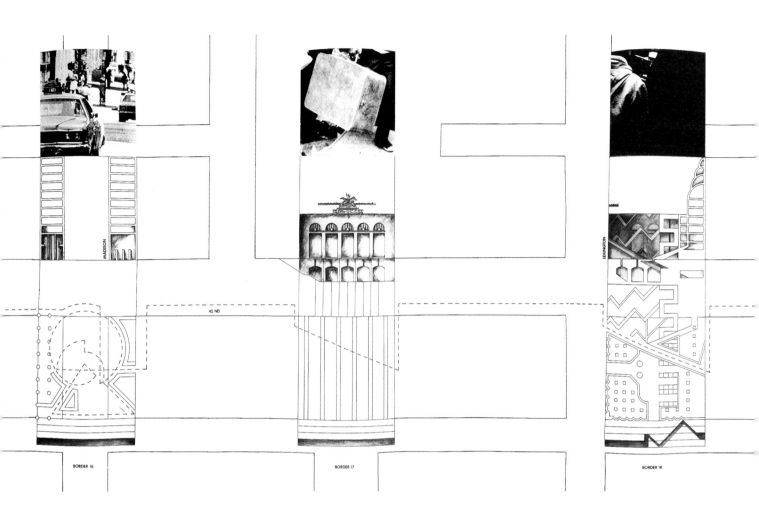

BORDER 16   BORDER 17   BORDER 18

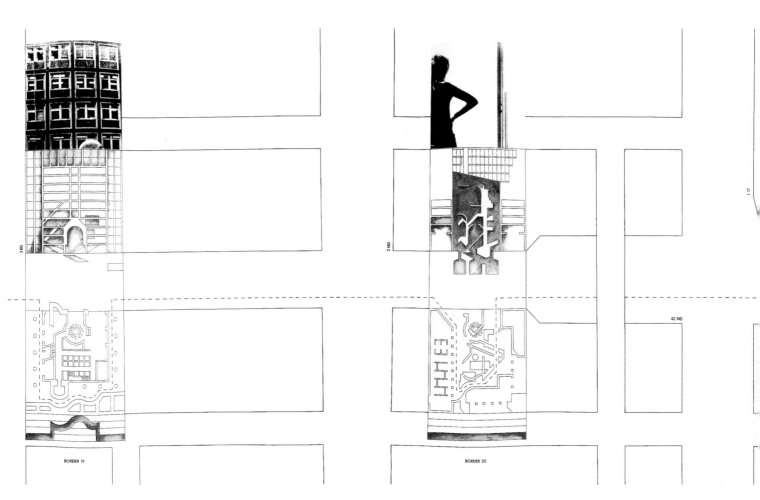

3RD

2ND

41

42 ND

BORDER 19

BORDER 20

BORDER 21

BORDER 22

BORDER 23

EAST RIVER

EPISODE 3: THE TOWER (THE FALL)

'The Fall . . . First it was
just a battered child, then
a row of cells, then a whole
tower. The wave of movement
spread, selective and sudden,
threatening to engulf the
whole city in a wave of chaos
and horror, unless. . . . But
what could she do . . . now that
the elevator ride had turned
into a chilling contest with
violent death? THE TOWER.'

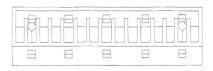

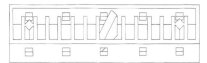

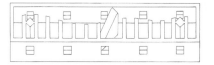

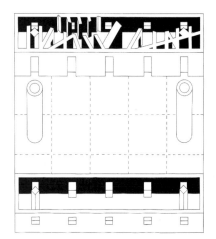

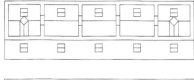

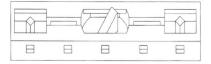

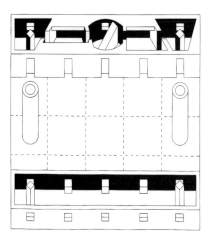

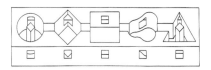

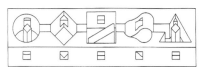

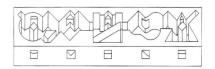

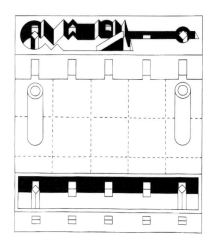

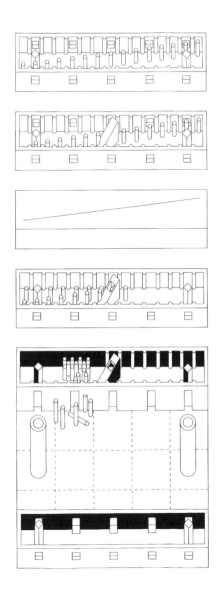

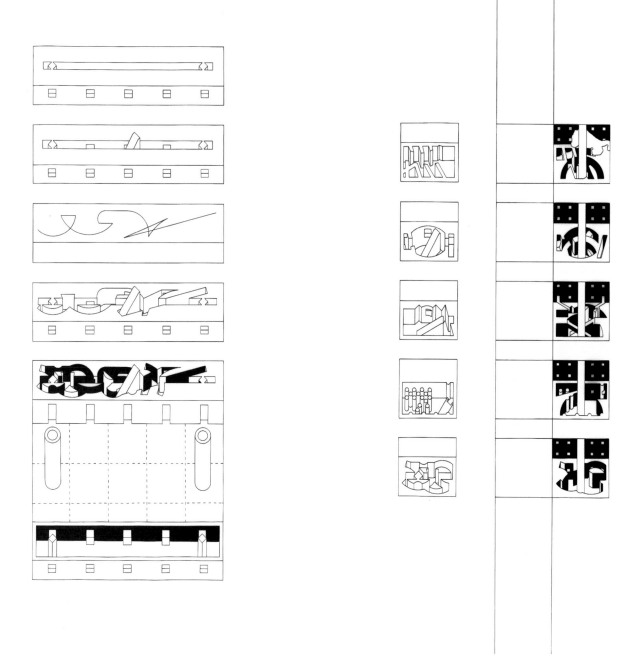

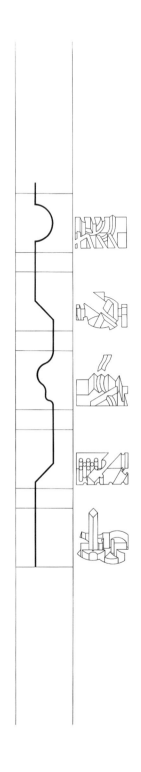

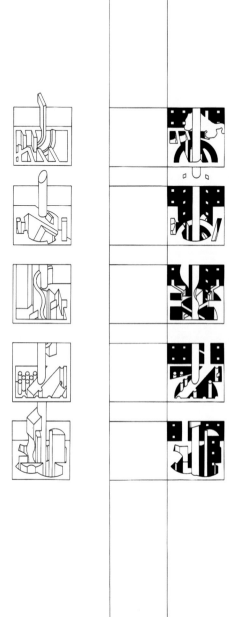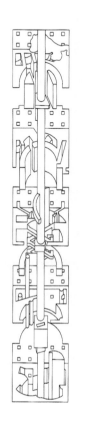

EPISODE 4: THE BLOCK

'Here is the Block, with
its loose yards and its
ruthless frames—where
well-dressed soldiers get
rich on acrobats' habits . . .
where fat football players
send you up for knowing the
wrong kind of strong-arm
dancers . . . where everything
you want belongs to somebody
else, and the only way to
get it is illegal, immoral,
or deadly. . . . THE BLOCK.'

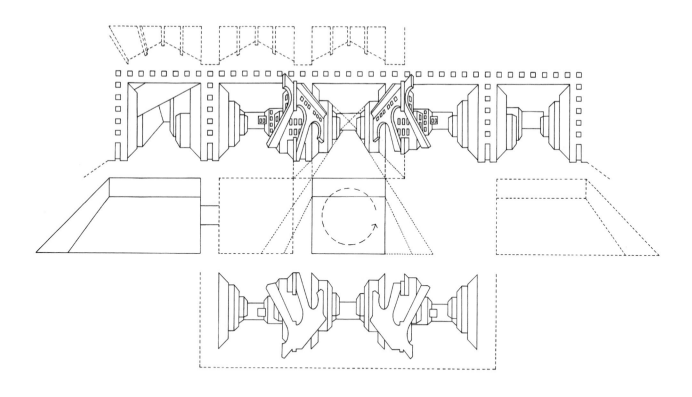

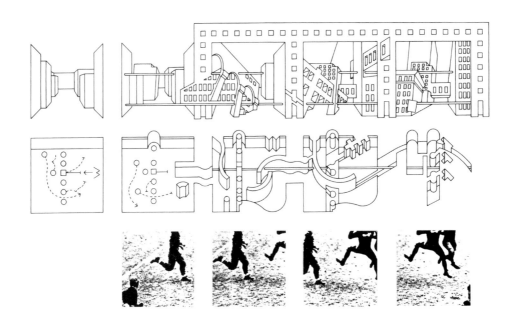

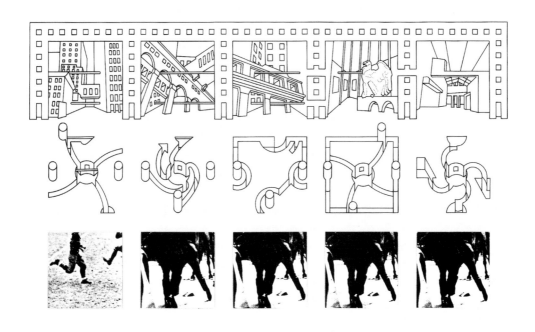

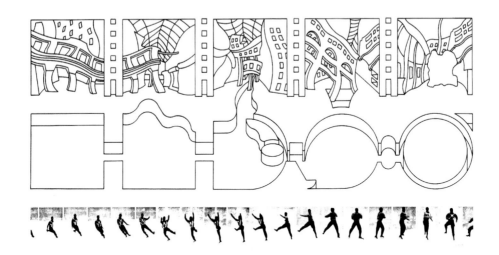

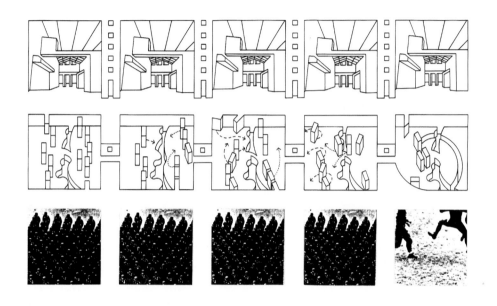

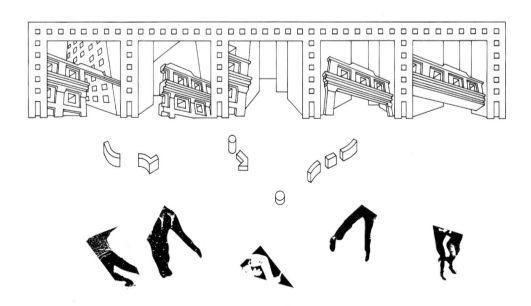

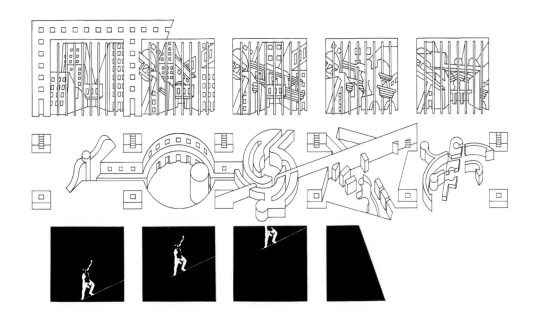

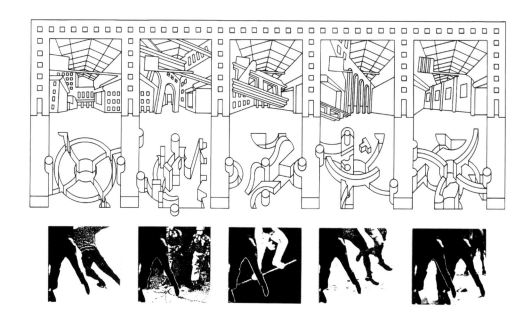

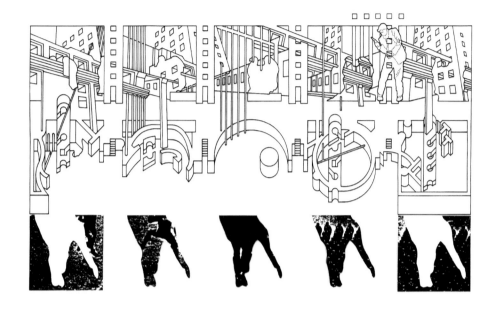

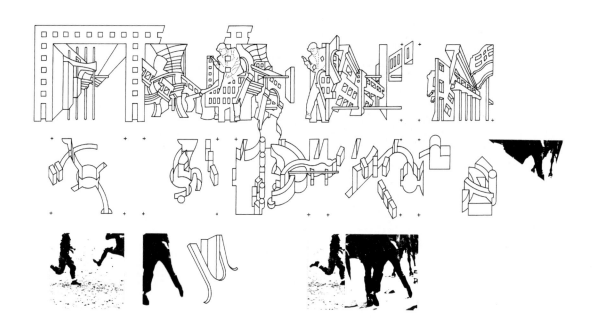

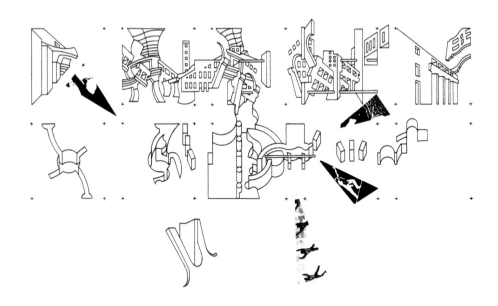

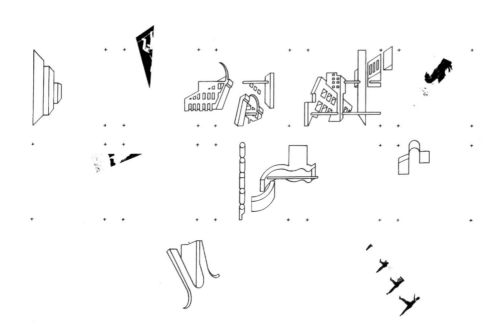

A fiercely gifted architect, Libeskind brings the weight of a lifelong immersion in philosophy, history, and intellectual esoterica to bear on each and every work of architecture he undertakes. For the first decade of his career, he gathered the attention of architects worldwide with a stunning succession of drawings and collages extraordinary in number, breadth, and imagination. Executed while Libeskind chaired the architecture program at the Cranbrook Academy of Art, *Micromegas* and *Chamber Works: Architectural Meditations on Themes from Heraclitus* date from the middle of that decade.

Named after Voltaire's satirical short story, Libeskind's *Micromegas* inhales in a single breath the history of modern drawing—from Giovanni Battista Piranesi through Vasily Kandinsky and on to Le Corbusier, Al Held, and John Hejduk—and exhales a gale of originality, one dizzying vertigo after another wrought from the interplay of line and sign. Better known in the form of a spectacular set of twelve prints, each titled with a literary reference to such works as Franz Kafka's "The Burrow," *Micromegas* began life as eleven untitled graphite-on-paper drawings (shown here). Although these would later become studies for the prints, the architect's signature and notation on each drawing indicate his confidence in them as works in their own right.

While far less dazzling than the prints, the pencil drawings are far more stirring. The no. 2 pencil line is so close in tone to the watercolor paper that it barely emerges from the page; one must approach closely to see the drawings even under favorable lighting. Because the range of values is so narrow, Libeskind could afford large zones of empty page without concern that the work would feel unfinished. While empty page is confined to the border of the chock-full prints, it trespasses unchecked into the pencil drawings. The zoo of torrid, deep-space graphic effects—rifts, clefts, fissures, fractures, crevices, arroyos, nooks, chasms, vortices, and holes that Libeskind sculpted in the *Micromegas* prints with his virtuoso linework—lies in the drawings against the dry shallow of the page with vertiginous result, the shallow further dessicated by the translucence of the graphite line. Because there is so much less blank page to fill in the drawings—even Libeskind's prodigious palette of graphic devices is finite—each is marked by a distinct theme and development. Thus the drawings avoid the tendency of the prints to merge into a monotony of interest.

DANIEL LIBESKIND

MICROMEGAS

1978

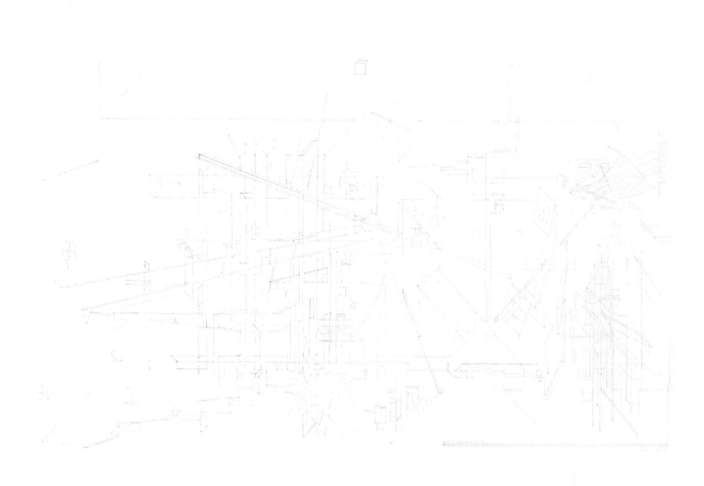

Commissioned for publication in the wake of the sensation over *Micromegas,* Libeskind executed the enigmatic drawings of *Chamber Works* reluctantly and in a different mood. Violent, erotic, angry, hilarious, they are nonetheless passion bound and chained, Apollo to *Micromegas*'s Dionysus. Such restraint is de rigueur, however, since they grapple with the deepest problem of how to join philosophy to architecture.

The collection of drawings divides into two sets of fourteen, each converging from an oriented field into a horizontal or vertical line. The ambiguity of that convergence is crucial. Either the field becomes a line as it recedes into graphic space—when the architect first exhibited the series, he set a scale of 1:20 for the first drawing and 1:200 for the last—or it evolves into a line over time. Existing neither simply in time nor space, the drawings effect a graphic escape from the regimes of both. They transcend time and space. Thus does Libeskind structure his turn on a problem that turned the head of philosopher Edmund Husserl: how do ideas transcend their parochial historical emergence to become timeless and placeless?

At first glance, the straight line seems an aboriginal miracle, landing on earth fully formed as world maker par excellence, the possibility of geometry, proportion, and measurement—of order as such. It delimits the horizon, the very limit of the world; the vertical, the orientation of rectitude (of the upright and normal) but also of ambition, sets the sky as limit. The irruptive force of *Chamber Works,* however, resides not so much in its admiration for the straight line but in its performance of the line's history. For on second thought, as we recall the Egyptians, the Greeks and Romans, Descartes, Newton, and Einstein, and indeed all of science and art and architecture, we realize that, like everything that exists, the line has a beginning and a genealogy.

Chamber Works offers an eccentric interpretation of that evolution. Its twenty-eight drawings form a score, one that must be played, however, for it cannot be read. There are cues to the performer: music, cloud chambers, Heraclitus, chess, cabala, gematria, doodles, even an echo of sonata form. But no keys, no tonal center, no reasons, no secrets to unlock. The gratings and grids, notational elements, zigs, zags, and curlicues all wander adrift; they make no sense, follow no logic of seriality or process, obey no law, honor no esoteric structure, construct no space, add up to nothing, depict nothing, mean nothing. They merely draw order out of chaos.

A genealogy, but also an ontogeny, for each of us, whatever our lot, must recapitulate that entire history for ourself, regrow so to speak our own personal lines. In so doing, we, like Libeskind, sustain the straight line and its two glorious postures—the horizontal and the vertical—as transcendentals even as we contribute to their evolution.

DANIEL LIBESKIND

CHAMBER WORKS: ARCHITECTURAL MEDITATIONS
ON THEMES FROM HERACLITUS

1983

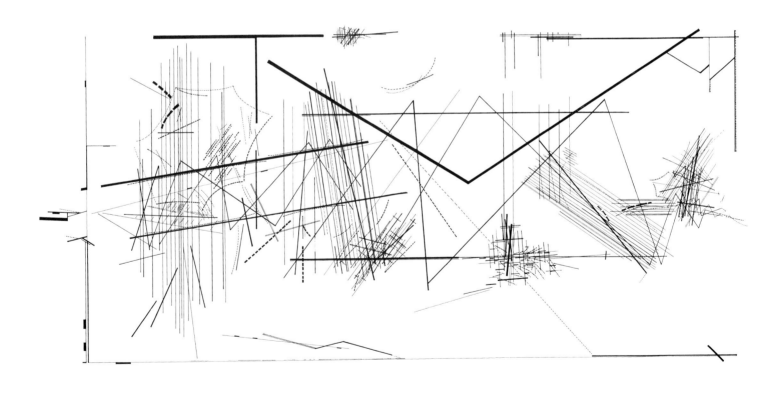

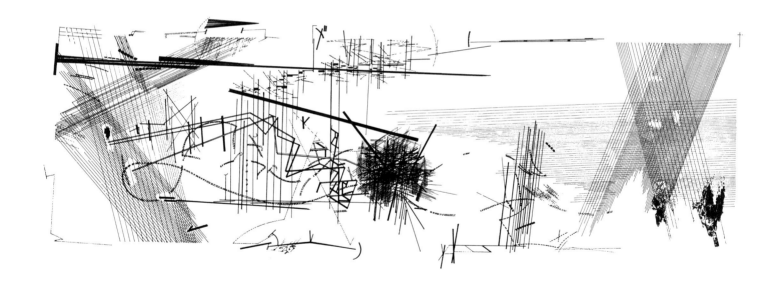

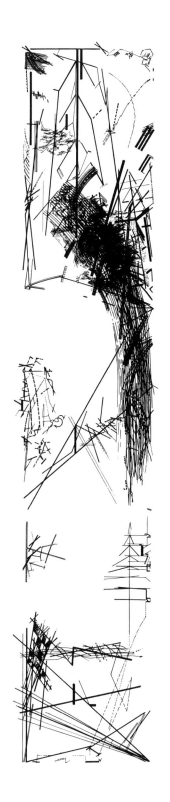

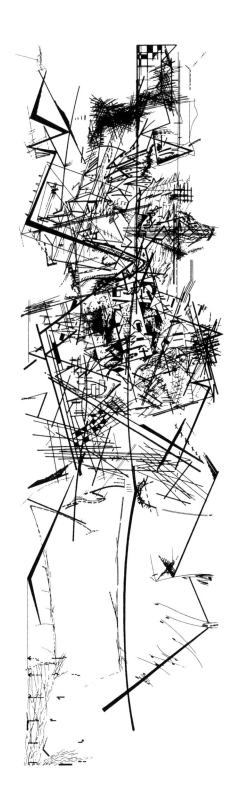

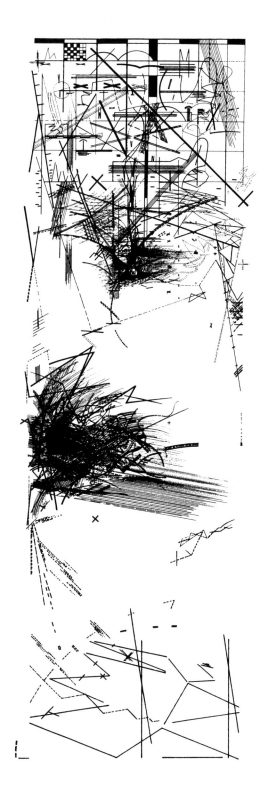

147

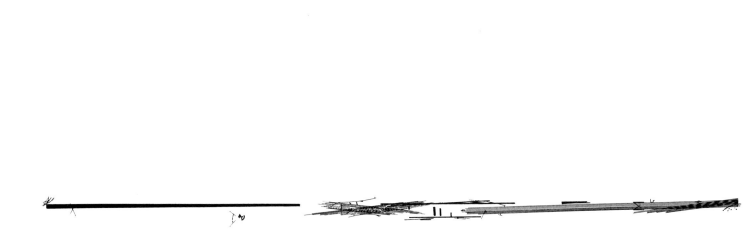

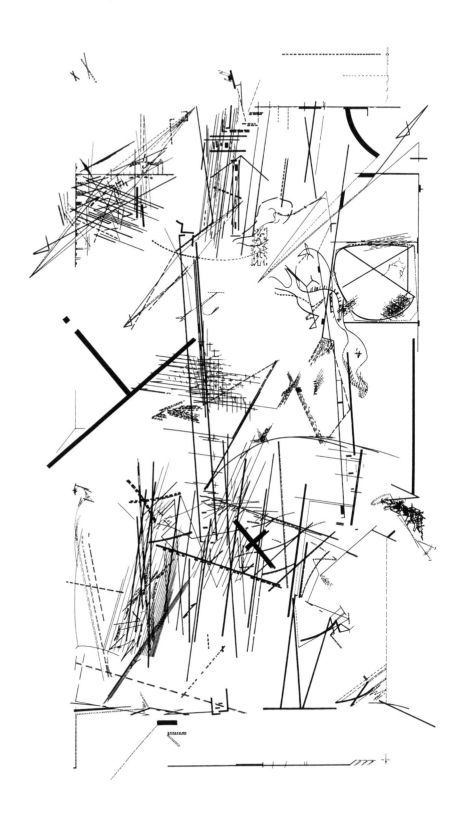

Beguiled by complex mechanisms, Thom Mayne inverts conventional
hierarchies by accentuating part over whole. For his own residence,
Mayne proposed to insert eleven found objects incongruously
into a generic frame house. The eleven steel machinery parts
were to be reworked into functional elements—staircase, fireplace,
shower—a characteristic tactic of "dead tech" architecture.
Denied financing, Mayne abandoned the project. He worked with
architect Andrew Zago to conceive drawings that captured the
subtleties of the original concept. How to draw a set of plans,
sections, and elevations that would capture the individuality of
each object and their curious correlations? A standard set of
drawings would dilute the rich complexities.

Straining the standards of architectural graphics to the
breaking point, Mayne's and Zago's ingenious solution employed two
graphic innovations. First, all sections and elevations are drawn
to a view oblique to a principal axis of the plan. For example,
rather than presenting a section of the building cut parallel to a
principal facade, the drawing shows the building sliced by a plane
oblique to a main facade, presenting internal relationships thus
not subordinated to the dominant geometry of the building. Second,
on every sheet Zago drew two interrelated treatments on the same
page: a $^3/_4$" = 1' plan, section, or elevation and a $^1/_2$" = 1' isometric
study of an object. Each sheet is conceived as an elevation of
the building, with the edge of the paper equated to the edge of the
building. This framework locates both the objects and the positions
of the diagrams; for example, the center line of the plan of the
loft floor sits on the page where the loft would occur in the
building. One object is studied in $^1/_2$" isometric per page, its
location also determined by its position in the building; on a
particular page, the relative positions of the other objects are
indicated by abstract two-dimensional notations. Each object has its
own character, and its skewed position within the spatial matrix
of the house responds to its function and its relationship with
the other objects. Zago ultimately drew just ten of the objects,
labeled A through J.

The texture of the drawings derives in part from Zago's
fascination with Daniel Libeskind's *Micromegas*; he had received
one of the prints as a gift just before beginning work on the
Sixth Street House drawings. The labyrinthine intricacy of the
works caused a sensation, and their intriguing spiderweb of lines
launched a style of complicated, multiview drawing. Unlike the
obtuse graphic hysteria they spawned, however, Mayne's and
Zago's ten drawings are models of cold precision and efficiency.
Their broad appeal encouraged Mayne to produce a color serigraph
version with printmaker John Nichols. Sales of these prints
helped sustain Mayne's office.

THOM MAYNE WITH ANDREW ZAGO

SIXTH STREET HOUSE

1986—87

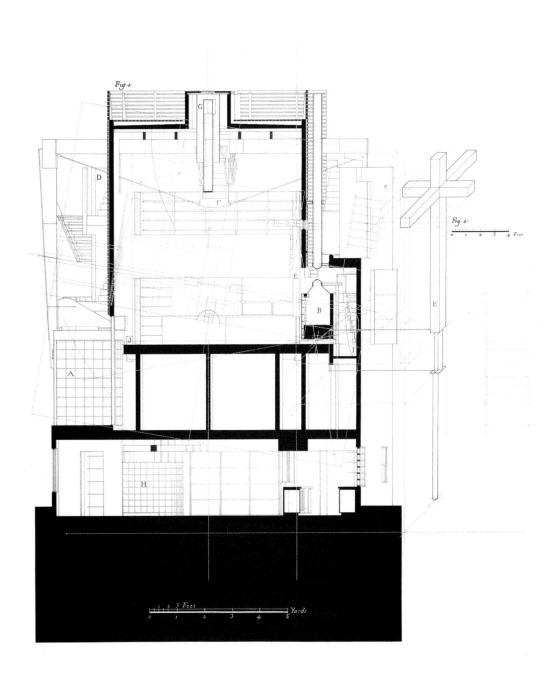

Fig. 1.

D

G

F

E

E

B

J

A

I

H

Fig. 2.

0   1   2   3   4 Feet

3 Feet

0   1   2   3   4   5 Yards

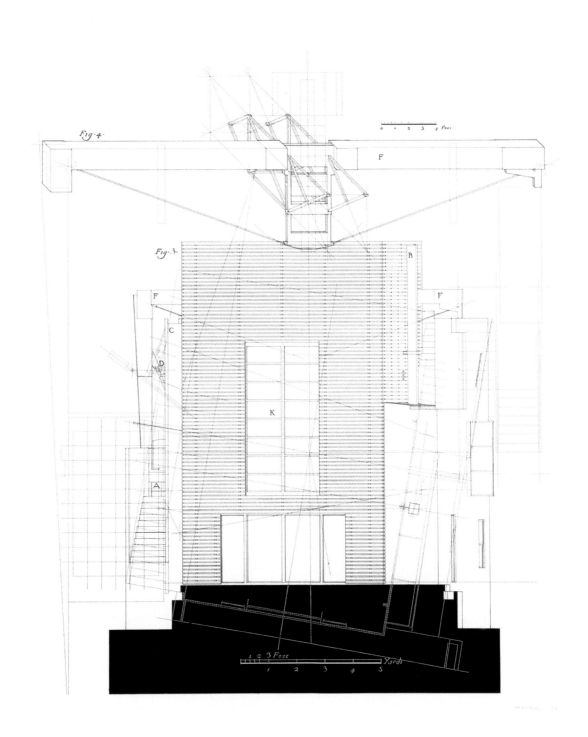

Fig. 4.

Fig. 3.

F

B

F   F

C

D

A

K

0 1 2 3 4 Feet

1 2 3 Foot

Yards

1   2   3   4   5

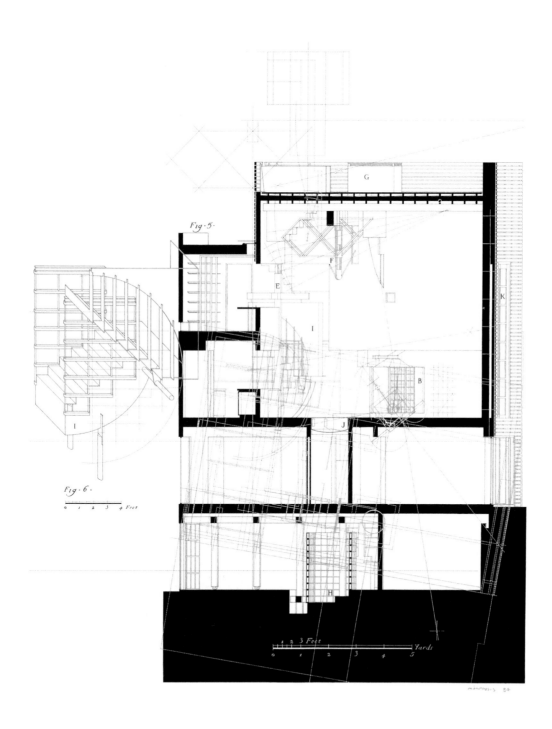

Fig · 5 ·

Fig · 6 ·

0   1   2   3   4 Feet

1 2 3 Feet

0   1   2   3   4   5

Yards

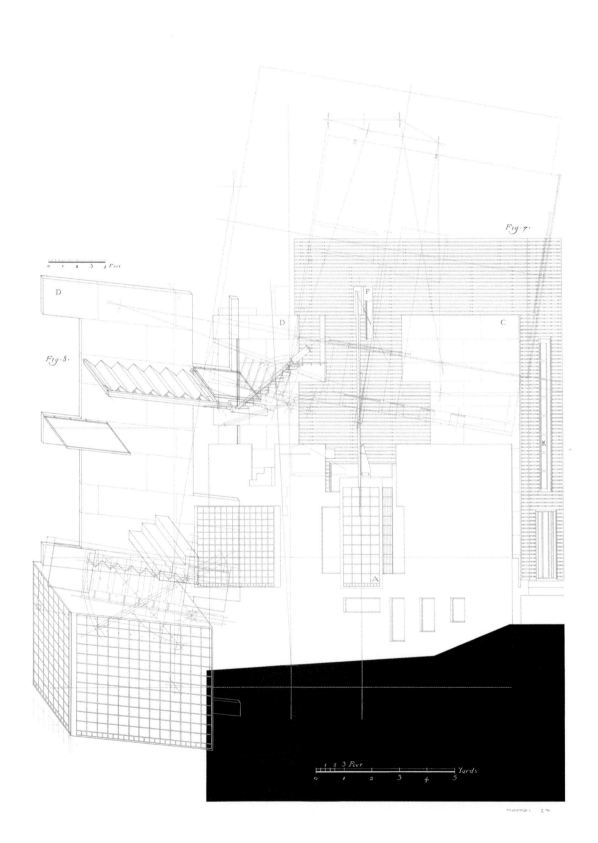

Fig. 7.

Fig. 8.

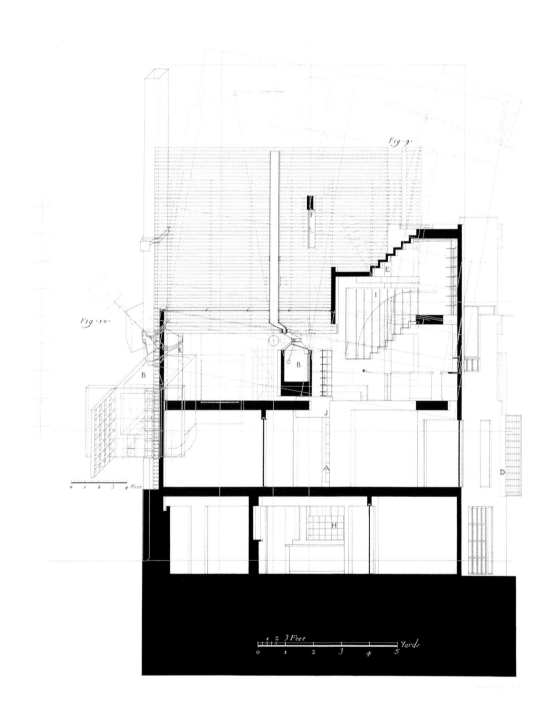

Fig · 9 ·

Fig · 10 ·

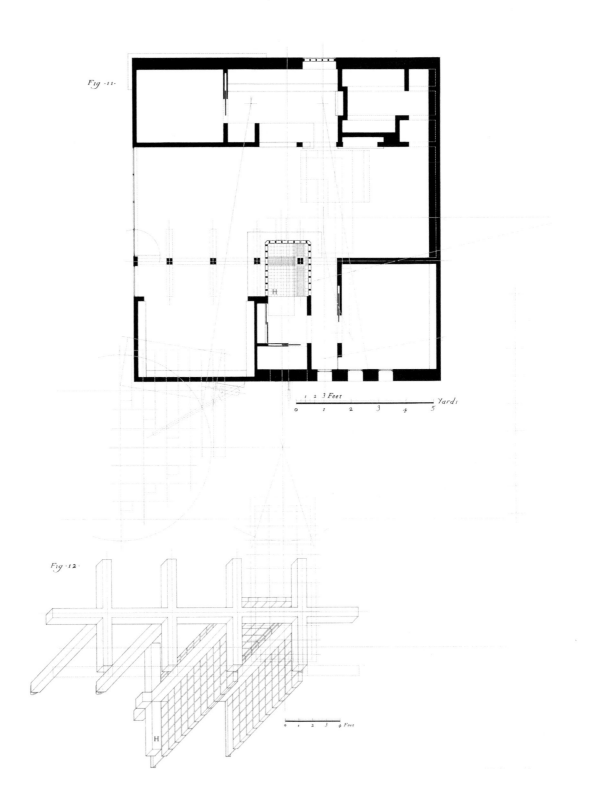

Fig ·11·

Fig ·12·

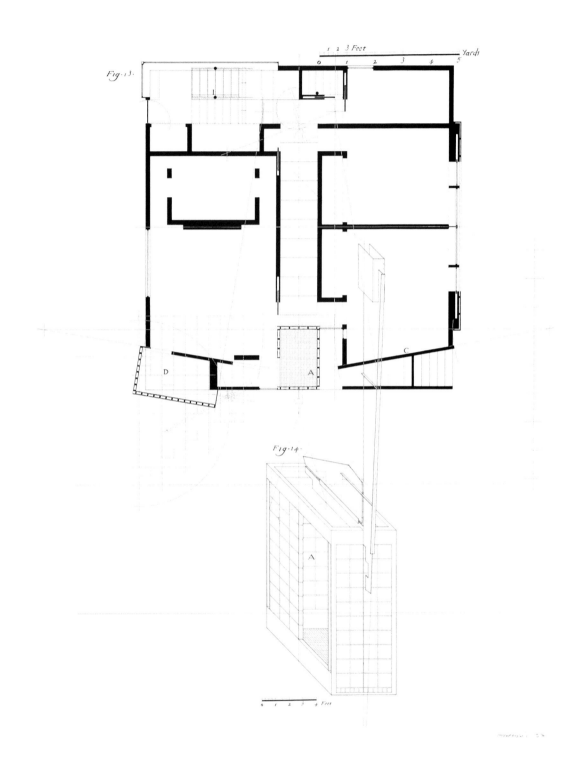

Fig. 13.

1 2 3 Feet

Yards
0   1   2   3   4   5

I

D   A   C

Fig. 14.

A

0   1   2   3   4 Feet

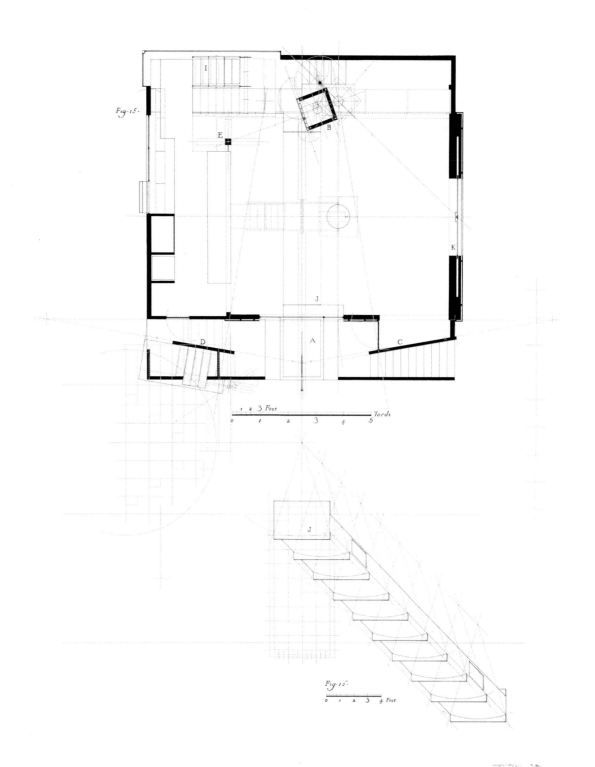

Fig·15·

Fig·16·

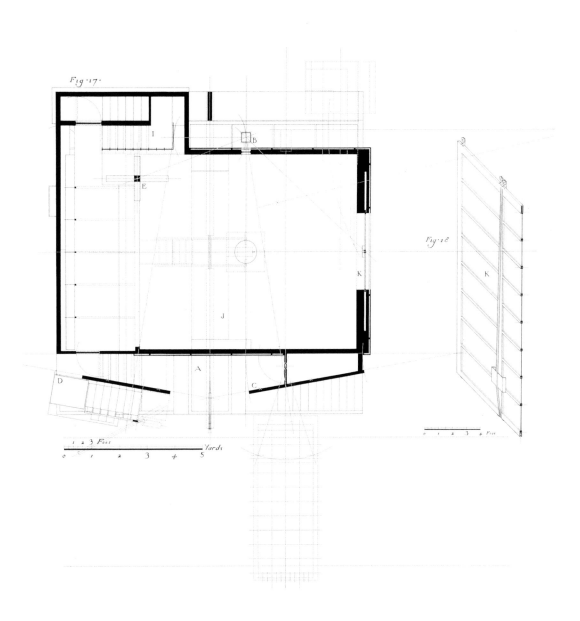

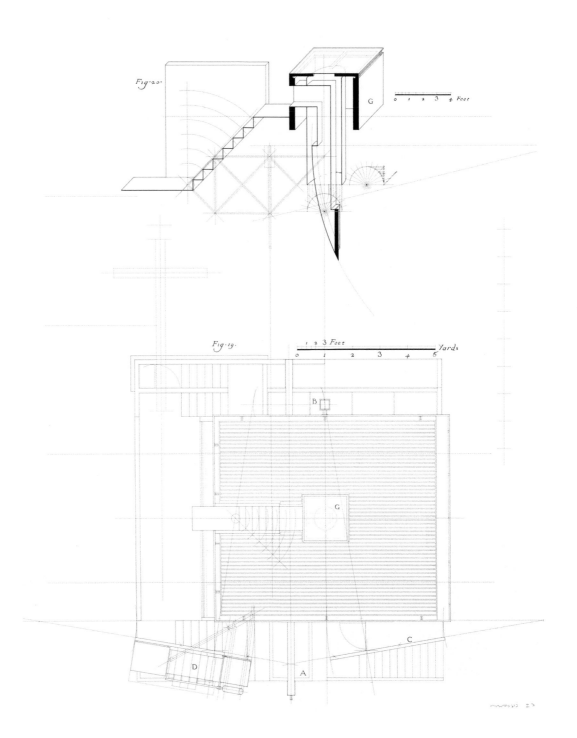

Fig. 20.

G

0 1 2 3 4 Feet

Fig. 19.

1 2 3 Feet

Yards
0   1   2   3   4   5

B

G

D

A

C

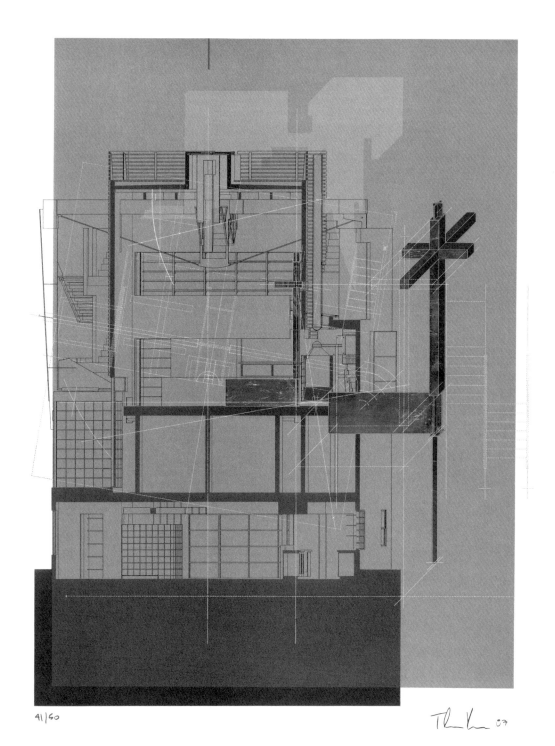

41/50

TH 07

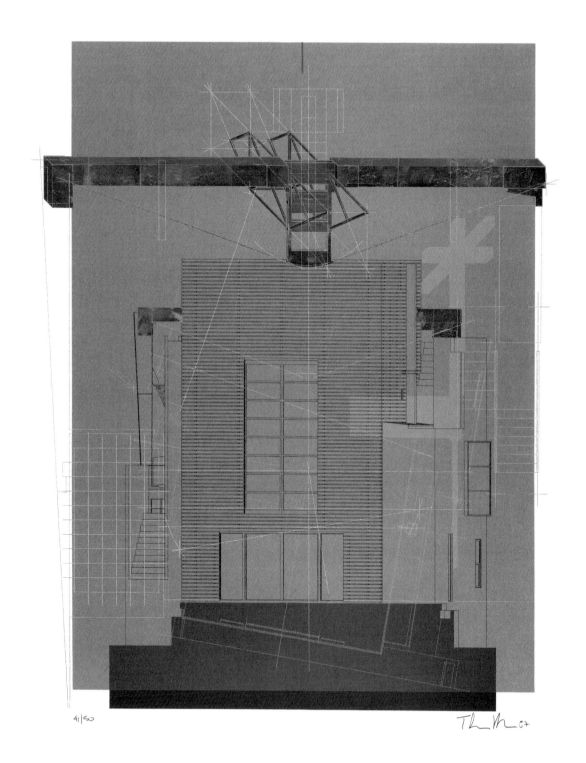

41/50

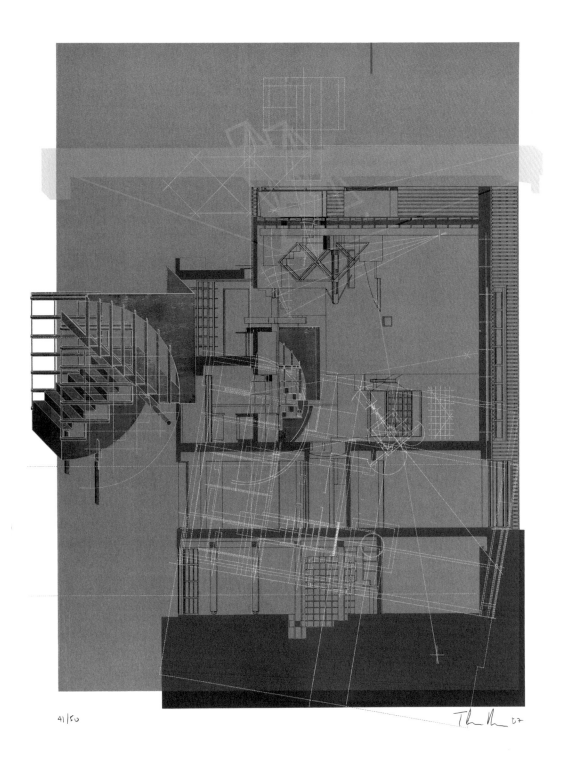

41/50

41/50

REM KOOLHAAS (Dutch, born 1944) and
ELIA ZENGHELIS (British, born Greece 1937) with
MADELON VRIESENDORP (Dutch, born 1945) and
ZOE ZENGHELIS (British, born Greece 1937)

EXODUS, OR THE VOLUNTARY PRISONERS OF ARCHITECTURE
1972

The Museum of Modern Art, New York
Patricia Phelps de Cisneros Purchase Fund, Takeo Ohbayashi
Purchase Fund, and Susan de Menil Purchase Fund

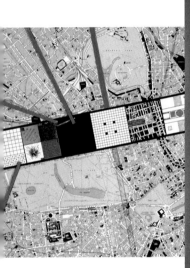

p. 16
Prologue
Gelatin silver photographs on board
16¼ x 11½" (41.3 x 29.2 cm)

p. 17
The Strip
Cut-and-pasted paper and painted paper with ink,
pen, and graphite on photolithograph (map of London)
19¾ x 25⅞" (50.2 x 65.7 cm)

p. 18
Exhausted Fugitives Led to Reception
Cut-and-pasted gelatin silver photographs
and photolithographs with ink, crayon,
and felt-tipped pen on paper
16 x 11½" (40.6 x 29.2 cm)

p. 19
The Strip
Cut-and-pasted paper with watercolor, ink, gouache,
and color pencil on gelatin silver photograph
16 x 19⅞" (40.6 x 50.5 cm)

p. 20
Training the New Arrivals
Cut-and-pasted photolithographs and
gelatin silver photograph on paper
10⅝ x 14½" (27 x 36.8 cm)

p. 21
The Reception Area
Gelatin silver photograph with color ink
10½ x 14½" (26.7 x 36.8 cm)

p. 22
The Central Area
Graphite and watercolor on paper
16⅜ x 11⅜" (41.6 x 28.9 cm)

p. 23
The Central Area
Graphite and watercolor on paper
11½ x 16⅜" (29.2 x 41.6 cm)

PETER EISENMAN (American, born 1932)

HOUSE VI
c. 1976

Built in Cornwall, Connecticut, House VI was completed in 1975.

pp. 36–49
Transformations
Zipatone and laminated colored paper with ink on paper
Each 19³/₄ x 23⁷/₈" (50.2 x 60.6 cm)
Delineators: Read Ferguson, Caroline Sidnam,
William Jackson, Randall Korman, and Rodney Knox
Collection Suzanne and Dick Frank

pp. 50 and 52–55
Cube Transformation Studies
Laminated colored paper with ink on paper
Each 20 x 19¹⁵/₁₆" (50.8 x 50.6 cm)
Peter Eisenman Archive, Collection Centre Canadien
d'Architecture/Canadian Centre for Architecture, Montreal

pp. 51, 56, and 57
Cube Transformation Studies
Collection unknown; photographs courtesy Peter Eisenman

Eight drawings from the *Cube Transformation Studies,*
on loan from the Peter Eisenman Archive, Collection
Centre Canadien d'Architecture/Canadian Centre for
Architecture, Montreal, are included in the exhibition
Perfect Acts of Architecture. Five of them are
reproduced in this catalogue. The other three have
been replaced by images of three drawings whose
whereabouts are unknown in order to illustrate
a more coherent sequence.

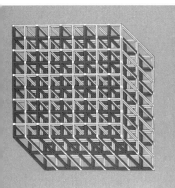

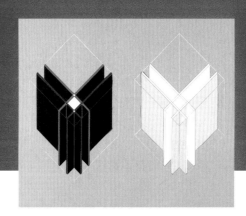

BERNARD TSCHUMI (Swiss and French, born Switzerland 1944)

THE MANHATTAN TRANSCRIPTS
1976—81

The Museum of Modern Art, New York
Purchase and partial gift of the architect in honor of Lily Auchincloss

p. 61
Introductory panel to *Episode 1: The Park,* 1980
Photographic reproduction with colored synthetic laminate
20 x 20" (50.8 x 50.8 cm)

pp. 62—73
Episode 1: The Park, 1976—77
Gelatin silver photographs
Each 14 x 18" (35.6 x 45.7 cm)

p. 75
Introductory panel to *Episode 2: The Street (Border Crossing),* 1980
Photographic reproduction with colored synthetic laminate
20 x 20" (50.8 x 50.8 cm)

pp. 77—84
Episode 2: The Street (Border Crossing), 1978
Ink, charcoal, graphite, cut-and-pasted photographic
reproductions, Letraset type, and color pencil on tracing paper
24" x 32'2" (61 x 980.4 cm)

p. 87
Introductory panel to *Episode 3: The Tower (The Fall),* 1980
Photographic reproduction with colored synthetic laminate
20 x 20" (50.8 x 50.8 cm)

pp. 88—93 left
Episode 3: The Tower (The Fall), 1979
Ink on tracing paper
Each 48 x 24" (121.9 x 61 cm)

p. 93 right
Episode 3: The Tower (The Fall), 1979
Ink and photographic reproductions on tracing paper
48 x 24" (121.9 x 61 cm)

p. 95
Introductory panel to *Episode 4: The Block,* 1980
Photographic reproduction with colored synthetic laminate
20 x 20" (50.8 x 50.8 cm)

pp. 96 and 98—109
Episode 4: The Block, 1980—81
Ink and cut-and-pasted gelatin silver photographs
on tracing paper
Each 19 x 31" (48.3 x 78.7 cm)

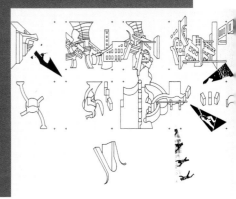

p. 97
Episode 4: The Block, 1980—81
Ink on tracing paper
19 x 31" (48.3 x 78.7 cm)

DANIEL LIBESKIND (American, born Poland 1946)

MICROMEGAS
1978

Graphite on paper
San Francisco Museum of Modern Art
Accessions Committee Fund: gift of Pam and Dick Kramlich,
Byron R. Meyer, Nancy and Steven Oliver, Leanne B. Roberts,
and Collectors Forum

p. 112
26 x 36¼" (66 x 92.1 cm)
Inscribed lower right in graphite: I. Libeskind 1978

p. 113
26 x 36¼" (66 x 92.1 cm)
Inscribed lower right in graphite: II. Libeskind 1978

p. 114
26 x 36¼" (66 x 92.1 cm)
Inscribed lower right in graphite: III. Libeskind 1978

p. 115
36¼ x 26" (92.1 x 66 cm)
Inscribed lower right in graphite: IV. Libeskind 1978

p. 116
36¼ x 26" (92.1 x 66 cm)
Inscribed lower right in graphite: V. Libeskind 1978

p. 117
36¼ x 26" (92.1 x 66 cm)
Inscribed lower right in graphite: VI. Libeskind 1978

p. 118
26 x 36¼" (66 x 92.1 cm)
Inscribed lower right in graphite: VII. Libeskind 1978

p. 119
36¼ x 26" (92.1 x 66 cm)
Inscribed lower right in graphite: VIII. Libeskind 1978

p. 120
36¼ x 26" (92.1 x 66 cm)
Inscribed lower right in graphite: IX. Libeskind 1978

p. 121
26 x 36¼" (66 x 92.1 cm)
Inscribed lower right in graphite: X. Libeskind 1978

p. 122
36¼ x 26" (92.1 x 66 cm)
Inscribed lower right in graphite: Libeskind 1978

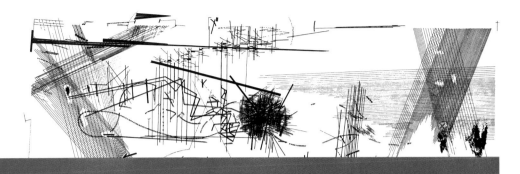

CHAMBER WORKS: ARCHITECTURAL MEDITATIONS ON THEMES FROM HERACLITUS
1983

Courtesy Studio Daniel Libeskind

pp. 126–52, even-numbered pages
Horizontal 14–1 (fourteen drawings)

pp. 127–53, odd-numbered pages
Vertical 1–14 (fourteen drawings)

Because the original drawings were lost, the
catalogue images were reproduced from the original
negatives. The works shown in the exhibition were
printed in 2000 from those negatives; the horizontal
works measure 22¼ x 30⅛" (56.5 x 76.5 cm), and
the vertical ones 30⅛ x 22¼" (76.5 x 56.5 cm).

THOM MAYNE (American, born 1944) with
ANDREW ZAGO (American, born 1958)
Morphosis, established Santa Monica, 1972

SIXTH STREET HOUSE
1986—87

A different version of Sixth Street House was built
in Santa Monica several years later.

Project team: Kim Groves, Charlie Scott, Andrew Zago,
Maya Shimoguchi, Joey Shimoda, and Tim Swischuk

pp. 156—65
Ink and graphite on Strathmore board
Each 40 x 30" (101.6 x 76.2 cm)
Delineators: Thom Mayne with Andrew Zago
Each inscribed lower right in graphite: Morphosis 87
San Francisco Museum of Modern Art
Accessions Committee Fund: gift of Jean Douglas,
Diane M. Heldfond, and Nancy and Steven Oliver

> p. 156
> *Sixth Street: Figure 2, 1986—87*
>
> p. 157
> *Sixth Street: Figure 4, 1986—87*
>
> p. 158
> *Sixth Street: Figure 6, 1986—87*
>
> p. 159
> *Sixth Street: Figure 8, 1986—87*
>
> p. 160
> *Sixth Street: Figure 10, 1986—87*
>
> p. 161
> *Sixth Street: Figure 12, 1986—87*
>
> p. 162
> *Sixth Street: Figure 14, 1986—87*
>
> p. 163
> *Sixth Street: Figure 16, 1986—87*
>
> p. 164
> *Sixth Street: Figure 18, 1986—87*
>
> p. 165
> *Sixth Street: Figure 20, 1986—87*

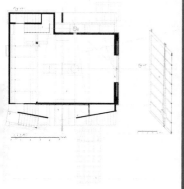

pp. 166—69
Serigraphs with metal foil on paper
Each 40 x 30" (101.6 x 76.2 cm)
Delineators: Thom Mayne with Selwyn Ting; printmaker: John Nichols
Edition: 41/50
The Museum of Modern Art, New York
Given anonymously

p. 166
Sixth Street: Figure 2, 1987
Inscribed lower left in graphite: 41/50;
inscribed lower right in graphite: Thom Mayne 87

p. 167
Sixth Street: Figure 4, 1987
Inscribed lower left in graphite: 41/50;
inscribed lower right in graphite: Thom Mayne 87

p. 168
Sixth Street: Figure 6, 1987
Inscribed lower left in graphite: 41/50;
inscribed lower right in graphite: Thom Mayne 87

p. 169
Sixth Street: Composite, 1990
Inscribed lower left in graphite: 41/50;
inscribed lower right in graphite: Thom Mayne 90

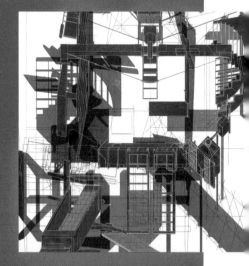

SELECTED BIBLIOGRAPHY

Rem Koolhaas and Elia Zenghelis with Madelon Vriesendorp and Zoe Zenghelis

EXODUS, OR THE VOLUNTARY PRISONERS OF ARCHITECTURE

Koolhaas, Rem, and Elia Zenghelis. "Exodus o i prigionieri volontari dell'architettura"/"Exodus or the Voluntary Prisoners of Architecture." *Casabella* 37, no. 378 (June 1973), pp. 42–45.

Office for Metropolitan Architecture, Rem Koolhaas, and Bruce Mau. *Small, Medium, Large, Extra-Large*. Ed. Jennifer Sigler. New York: The Monacelli Press, 1995.

Peter Eisenman

HOUSE VI

Eisenman, Peter. *Houses of Cards*. Essays by Eisenman, Rosalind Krauss, and Manfredo Tafuri. New York: Oxford University Press, 1987.

Frank, Suzanne. *Peter Eisenman's House VI: The Client's Response*. New York: Watson-Guptill Publications, Whitney Library of Design, 1994.

Bernard Tschumi

THE MANHATTAN TRANSCRIPTS

Tschumi, Bernard. *The Manhattan Transcripts*. New York: St. Martin's Press; London: Academy Editions, 1981.

Daniel Libeskind

MICROMEGAS

Libeskind, Daniel. *Between Zero and Infinity: Selected Projects in Architecture*. New York: Rizzoli International Publications, 1981.

CHAMBER WORKS: ARCHITECTURAL MEDITATIONS ON THEMES FROM HERACLITUS

Libeskind, Daniel. *Chamber Works: Architectural Meditations on Themes from Heraclitus*. Essays by Peter Eisenman, Kurt Forster, John Hejduk, and Aldo Rossi. London: Architectural Association, 1983.

Thom Mayne with Andrew Zago

SIXTH STREET HOUSE

Wagner, George, ed. *Thom Mayne, Sixth Street House*. Cambridge, Mass.: Harvard University Graduate School of Design, 1989.

WEXNER CENTER FOR THE ARTS